STRESS

Less

Four Weeks to
More Abundant Living

By

Margie Hesson

Stress Less
Four Weeks to More Abundant Living

Copyright © 1999 by Abingdon Press

Scripture quotations are from the New Revised Standard Version of the Bible, copyright © 1989 by the Division of Christian Education, National Council of the Churches of Christ in the United States of America. Used by permission.

References:
Apples of Gold, compiled by Jo Petty and published by The C. R. Gibson Company.
The Breath of Life, by Ron DelBene. Published by Upper Room Books, 1992.
Health Yourself!, by Margie Hesson. Published by Abingdon Press, 1995.
High Level Wellness: An Alternative to Doc, Drugs, and Disease, by Donald B. Ardell.
Laugh Again, by Charles Swindoll. Published by Word Publishing, 1992.
Pack up Your Gloomies in a Great Big Box, by Barbara Johnson. Published by Word Publishing, 1993.
The Relaxation Response, by Herbert Benson. Published by Avon Books, 1975.
The Spirit of Synergy, by Robert Keck. Published by Parthenon Press, 1980.
Stages of Change in the Modification of Problem Behaviors, by J. Prochaska and C. DiClemente in Progress in Behavior Modification, 28, 183-218, 1992.
The Stress Concept Today, by Hans Selye in I. Kutash et al., eds., *The Handbook on Stress and Anxiety,* published by Jossey-Boss, 1989.

ISBN 0-687-02942-2

99 00 01 02 03 04 05 06 07 08—10 9 8 7 6 5 4 3 2 1

ACKNOWLEDGMENTS

My husband, Jim—for your never-ending love and for showing me by your example what is possible by setting a goal and trusting in God for help and guidance. Thanks for serving as contributing author for *Stress Less.*

David—for your keen insights and for sharing your computer expertise with your old mom. If it weren't for you, I'd still be trying to figure out how to format the disk.

Jenny—for a wonderful memory of flying to New York together and spending the whole time helping me work through the ideas for *Stress Less.* Your creative and intelligent perspective influenced the words I wrote. You make a mother proud.

Stress Less reviewers—Dr. Kay Foland, Dr. Larry Tentinger, the Reverend Kip Roozen, Dr. Mary Lou Mylant, Jennifer Hesson, and Dr. Jim Hesson. I respect each of you for your insight and expertise. My sincere thanks for sharing your time and wisdom.

My friend, Mary Ellen Fawcett—for the hours you spent searching the scriptures and reviewing books for "stress less" inspirations. The way you value the everyday blessings in life is an example of more abundant living for all who know you.

Shauna Bruce—for all your great ideas and your spiritual insights. You are an inspiration and example of spiritual health put into action. You are a special person, Shauna.

Dr. Alice Weldon—for the time we shared at the beach brainstorming about ideas for this book. I value your wisdom and friendship.

Emily Squires—for instilling in me a confidence of believing in myself and for living your life as an example of Christian love. Thanks, Mom.

My sisters, Pat Witkowski and Peg Jones—for listening to me babble on about my ideas and for just always being in my life.

Bud Solverson—for teaching me the value of hard work.

The Reverend Millsaps Dye—for your encouragement and support from the very beginning. You got me started, friend.

South Dakota State University, College of Nursing students and faculty —for writing "stress stories" and encouraging me to write *Stress Less.*

Mary Johannes—for your support, encouragement and positive attitude. You have been great to work with. *Stress Less* would not have happened without you.

CONTENTS

Section 1 Chapter 1

CARING FOR YOURSELF

*S*it up straight. Take a long, very deep breath in through your nose. Blow out forcefully through your mouth. Let your shoulders fall. Raise your eyebrows. Smile. I'll bet you feel better already.

Our creator tells us in John 10:10: "I came that they may have life, and have it abundantly." Yet every day we see people who are just surviving, not thriving; not experiencing the energizing joy that comes from combining personal action with the assurance that God will care for them. My hopes and prayers in writing *Stress Less* are that you can use this information for a more abundant life.

You will discover how to
- Achieve greater health, greater happiness, greater peace of mind
- Feel calm and peaceful, yet energized
- Stop wasting energy on worry and anger
- Take control of your stress and enjoy the process

Think of reading these chapters as the beginning of an exciting journey to a place you have never been before. A place where you feel balanced, contented, and peaceful. Close your eyes and imagine for a moment the feeling of peace and contentment, the feeling of letting go of the stress, anger, fear, and worry in your life. Not only can you go to this place, you can choose to stay—to live every day of your life with the happiness and wholeness that is God's will for you.

So, let the journey begin. In these first seven chapters you will learn about caring for yourself, the process of making changes in your life, the importance of your perceptions and expectations, and how to achieve balance in your life.

In the past few decades we have discovered beyond a doubt that the mind has a tremendous impact on the body. How you think—your beliefs, your attitudes, your emotions—and the behaviors you choose affect you for good or for ill.

Consider these questions: Can you *decide* to be happy, to live your life with joy and peace? Can it really be that simple—as simple as making a decision to change? What about the overwhelming pressures on your time? What about the sorrow you feel from a loved one's illness? What about your disappointment that life is not quite unfolding as you planned? What about the violence, the poverty, the sadness you see all around?

Yes, it is that simple. A change in consciousness and trusting in God produces amazing results. You can *decide* how you will deal with the challenges of life. It is not that these disappointments and sad things will go away. What will change is your way of thinking about them and your ability to cope with these challenges. Perhaps you have heard the saying, "Life is 10 percent what happens to you and 90 percent how you react to it."

It is simple, but not easy. You must learn new ways of thinking. You must practice new ways of dealing with stress in your life. You must trust in God for direction. You must make conscious and deliberate choices.

You must *care* for yourself. If you have ever flown in an airplane you have heard this advice, "Put your own oxygen mask on first before assisting others." Caring for yourself is like putting your oxygen mask on. To help others you must take care of yourself, yet we sometimes feel guilty for taking time for ourselves.

Here is something important to think about. *Does putting yourself first feel like selfishness or self-respect?* You may be so busy working and caring for your spouse, your boss, your children, your friends, your parents, or your church that you feel guilty taking time for yourself.

Think about this scripture: "Do you not know that your body is a temple of the Holy Spirit within you, which you have from God, and that you are not your own? For you were bought with a price; therefore glorify God in your body" (I Corinthians 6:19-20). God wants you to care for yourself and to treat yourself with respect. Give yourself permission to feel good about taking time for yourself. As you read *Stress Less* you will be glorifying God by learning to care for your body, mind, and spirit.

I sometimes have difficulty accepting the promise that God loves me no matter what I do or think or say. Yet I know it is true. What a wonderful, stress-relieving promise that is. When you look in the mirror, do you like the person you see? Do you see yourself as a person of worth and value? Are you proud of yourself? Do you respect yourself? Do you love yourself as God loves you?

If you think you do not have time for yourself, to stop and smell the roses, think again. Yes, your life is hectic and the pressures are many. Sure you are busy taking care of a family, working, being involved in your community, or some combination of these things. But that is exactly why you must take care of yourself and learn to cope with the stress in your life.

To keep a lamp burning, you must keep putting oil in it. Learning to stress less is like putting oil in your lamp. It is a gift you give yourself to keep your light shining, and your light will benefit all those around you.

Close your eyes and pray this simple prayer, "God, thank you for letting me be me. Help me to love and care for myself as you love and care for me. Amen."

Message to Remember
It is right and it is good to take care of yourself.

Start Today
Take some quiet time for yourself. Think of it as putting oil in your lamp so you can keep burning. Copy Psalm 23 on an index card. Read this scripture twice today. Sit quietly for five minutes after you finish reading.

Evening Reflection

What would you *most* like to achieve from reading *Stress Less*? Jot down the outcome you want.

Do you think you can decide to be happy and peaceful? Is it in your control? If not, who is in control of how you think and what you do?

Think of one word that comes to your mind from reading Psalm 23.

Before you go to bed tonight read and reflect on Philippians 4:8-9: "Finally, beloved, whatever is true, whatever is honorable, whatever is just, whatever is pure, whatever is pleasing, whatever is commendable, if there is any excellence and if there is anything worthy of praise, think about these things. Keep on doing the things that you have learned and received and heard and seen in me, and the God of peace will be with you."

THE LORD IS MY SHEPHERD

The LORD is my shepherd, I shall not want. | He makes me lie down in green pastures; | he leads me beside still waters; | he restores my soul. | He leads me in right paths for his name's sake. | Even though I walk through the darkest valley, | I fear no evil; | for you are with me; | your rod and your staff— | they comfort me. | You prepare a table before me in the presence of my enemies; | you anoint my head with oil; my cup overflows. | Surely goodness and mercy shall follow me | all the days of my life, | and I shall dwell in the house of the LORD | my whole life long.

(Psalm 23:1-6)

Brian was struggling to find happiness in his life. He thought that by now he would have figured things out; that he would feel some sense of meaning and purpose in his life. It just wasn't there. Brian was forty-four and married with three children. He had a good job but he thought by this stage of his life he would be better off financially. He and his wife both worked but had not been able to save, and their oldest child was nearing college age. With his wife throwing hints about a new house and their car about to turn over 100,000 miles, Brian was beginning to feel a sense of panic. He felt stressed and unappreciated. The words to an old song kept repeating in Brian's mind, "Is that all there is? Is that all there is?"

I had asked people in the couples group at church to share their stress stories. As Brian shared his story with the group, others nodded their heads in understanding. While our circumstances were all different, we could each relate to Brian's feelings of frustration and stress. Next I asked the group members to share one thing that had helped them deal with the stress. This is what Brian shared:

I had always found the 23rd Psalm to be comforting. It wasn't until I was going through this difficult time and a friend suggested that I read this scripture at least twice a day that I truly experienced the feeling of peace and the blessing that is promised here. I didn't feel the comforting peace immediately. With each reading, and as my mind cleared of other distractions, I began to find meaning that I hadn't seen before. I could feel myself relaxing and surrendering to the message. I came to trust that God was there with me every day to guide and direct me. I received the strength to deal with the problems and the assurance to let go of what I couldn't change. I still carry Psalm 23 in my billfold and take time every day to read the promise.

There is something special about Psalm 23. Read the words slowly and reflect on each sentence. Try reading the scripture as a prayerful meditation. Memorize the verses so you can close your eyes and visualize. Picture yourself resting in a green field and walking beside beautiful still waters.

"...He restores my soul." I find this phrase especially comforting. I am reminded of how we start out as children with our souls intact. Along the way we change. We may become cynical, we may stop loving ourselves, and we may experience brokenness. But just like old, broken-down furniture, we can be restored. As Jesus says in Matthew 18:3: "Truly I tell you, unless you change and become like children, you will never enter the kingdom of heaven." The image of being restored—made new again—is a comforting image.

I'm reminded of this story:

Ice Cream Is Good for the Soul

Last week I took my children to a restaurant. My six-year-old son asked if he could say grace. As we bowed our heads he said, "God is good. God is great. Thank you for the food, and I would thank you even more if mom gets us ice cream for dessert. And liberty and justice for all! Amen!"

Along with the laughter from the other customers, nearby I heard a woman remark, "That's what's wrong with this country. Kids today don't know how to pray. Asking God for ice cream! Why, I never!"

Hearing this, my son burst into tears and asked me, "Did I do it wrong, Mommy?" As I held him and assured him that he had done a terrific job and God was certainly not mad at him, an elderly gentleman approached the table. He winked at my son and said, "I happen to know that God thought that was a great prayer." "Really?" my son asked. "Cross my heart." Then in a theatrical whisper he added (indicating the woman whose remark had started this whole thing), "Too bad she never asks God for ice cream. A little ice cream is good for the soul sometimes."

Naturally, I bought my kids ice cream at the end of the meal. My son stared at his for a moment and then did something I will remember the rest of my life. He picked up his sundae and without a word walked over and placed it in front of the woman. With a big smile he told her, "Here, this is for you. Ice cream is good for the soul sometimes, and my soul is good already." (Source unknown)

Managing stress is about the peace that is yours from restoring your soul. It is about lying down in green pastures and walking beside still waters; about fearing no evil; about feeling the comfort of your Savior; about your cup overflowing.

Message to Remember
God will restore your soul and comfort you.

Start Today
Read Psalm 23 twice today. Reflect in prayerful meditation on the promise that it makes. Try inserting your own name as you read. For example, "The Lord is Margie's shepherd, she shall not want." Sit quietly for five minutes after reciting the scripture.

Evening Reflections
Imagine God actually talking to you when you insert your name in Psalm 23.

Which sentence do you find the most comforting? Why?

"By day the LORD commands his steadfast love, / and at night his song is with me, / a prayer to the God of my life" (Psalm 42:8). Let your last thoughts before you fall asleep tonight be Psalm 23.

$\mathscr{B}$LESSED BALANCE

May the God of peace himself sanctify you entirely; and may your spirit and soul and body be kept sound and blameless at the coming of our Lord Jesus Christ. The one who calls you is faithful, and will do this.
(1 Thessalonians 5:23-24)

$\mathscr{B}$ody, mind, and spirit; all three are important when you consider stress. Think of a three-legged stool. With all three legs in place you have a very well-balanced and stable seat, but if you remove one of the legs what happens? It is very easy to lose your balance and tip over. We had a one-legged stool that we used for milking cows on the Wisconsin farm where I grew up. One slap in the face from a cow's tail was enough to send me flying. The point is, you need balance for a stable, less fragile life. Being healthy in body, mind, and spirit provides you with the solid foundation you need to deal with the challenges and stress we all experience. When you are balanced, you are able to cope in a healthy manner.

Think of the athletes who spend hours, days, and years tuning their bodies. Yet a strong and healthy body may come at the expense of mental, emotional, or spiritual neglect. Think of the class valedictorian. Having the highest IQ is no guarantee of physical, spiritual, or social health. The key to well-being is in maintaining balance in body, mind, and spirit.

Every day you either grow or you stagnate—physically, emotionally, and spiritually. Think about your physical health.

What do you do to stay healthy physically? Think next of your emotional health. What do you do to stay healthy emotionally? Think about your spiritual health. What do you do to stay healthy spiritually? All three dimensions must be balanced for optimal well-being. We will cover physical and emotional health as it relates to stress in the coming chapters, but now we will focus on the importance of a healthy spirit. Human spirituality is the foundation of a peace-filled life.

My friend Shauna has a healthy spirit:

As a twenty-four-year-old, college graduate born with spina bifida, I have had much continual stress due to my disability. While growing up, I was a joyful and bubbly person. This was because of my belief in the Lord and my wonderful family and friends. They never saw me as disabled.

However, in my later years of school I developed an eating disorder due to my feelings of worthlessness and inferiority. This was even more stress added to my life. Fortunately, I began to attend church. I met people who prayed for me and showed me the word of God. Through this love and support, I began to see God's truth about myself. God's word tells me that I am accepted in the beloved. I am chosen by God and nothing will separate me from his love.

However, most importantly, God has recently revealed to me that I am not a victim of my circumstances. Despite how difficult my disability or life's situations may seem, I am more than an overcomer in all situations. God's word promises: "Whatever is born of God conquers the world" (1 John 5:4). I am not a victim of a cruel infirmity. None of God's children are victims of any situation, because we can overcome anything when he is in us.

I may not be able to control my disability but, through Jesus Christ, neither does my disability any longer control me or my view of myself. God's love for me is unconditional and everlasting, regardless of the abilities of my physical body.

Most of you are aware of the leading causes of death in the United States: heart and vascular disease, cancer, lung disease, accidents, suicide, homicide. You probably also are aware of some of the lifestyle habits that lead to many diseases: tobacco, diet, sedentary lifestyle, alcohol abuse. But what we often fail to consider are the underlying spiritual factors that greatly influence our lifestyle choices: loneliness, depression, low self-esteem, lack of meaning and purpose, feelings of hopelessness. Unhealthy lifestyle choices are often symptoms of underlying spiritual distress.

When we address only the symptoms it is like controlling weeds. If we cut off the top of the weed it will keep coming back. We must pull up the weed by the roots or it will keep cropping up. If we address only the physical and emotional dimensions of our health and fail to deal with the underlying spiritual dis-ease, the problems will keep coming back, and like weeds, they will spread all around.

What does it mean to be spiritually healthy? Larry Chapman, spiritual health editor for the *American Journal of Health Promotion* writes, "Optimal spiritual health is the ability to develop our spiritual nature to its fullest potential. This would include our ability to discover and articulate our own basic purpose in life, learn how to experience love, joy, peace and fulfillment, and how to help ourselves and others achieve their full potential."

Your spirituality gives you direction and purpose in your quest for a balanced life. The most expensive house, the biggest muscles, the highest IQ, and the most friends are meaningless unless they are considered from a higher perspective. Spiritual well-being provides you with the *why* for caring for yourself. When you see yourself as a valuable child of God, your quest for a healthy body, mind, and spirit takes on a whole new meaning.

Strive to achieve balance in your life every day. Resist allowing the urgent to take over the important. Ask yourself what is truly important in your life. What guides the decisions and choices you make every day?

Real peace comes to you when you know that as a child of God your life has meaning and purpose; when you are rooted and grounded in God. Put God first and you will have peace in your life. It's a spiritual issue.

Message to Remember
A healthy spirit is the foundation of a peace-filled life.

Start Today
Complete the Spiritual Wellness Assessment and Worksheet on the next page.

Evening Reflection
Look over your Spiritual Wellness Assessment. What did you learn?

Who comes to your mind when you think of a spiritually healthy person? What is it about this person that makes you think of him or her as spiritually healthy? Write down the person's name and the qualities or characteristics the person demonstrates.

What can you do to grow spiritually? Would doing any of these things help you deal with stress more effectively?

Think about the relationship between spirituality and stress.

SPIRITUAL WELLNESS ASSESSMENT

Instructions: In front of each item choose one of the following:
S = I'm doing *superior* in this area of my spiritual life
SS = I'm doing *so-so* or ok in this area, but things could be a lot better
NS = I *need strengthening* in this area

_____ I have a deeply held belief system or personal theology.

_____ I have faith in a higher power.

_____ Even during difficult times, I have a sense of hope.

_____ My spiritual beliefs help me remain calm and strong during times of stress.

_____ I feel a sense of connection to other people.

_____ I am able to forgive people who have done me wrong.

_____ I seek experiences with nature and reflect on nature's contribution to my quality of life.

_____ I find comfort in the practice of spiritual rituals (prayer, music, meditation, etc.).

_____ I feel loved.

_____ I am able to express my love for others.

_____ I respect the diversity of spiritual expression and am tolerant of those whose beliefs differ from my own.

_____ My life has meaning and purpose.

_____ My inner strength is related to my belief in a higher power.

_____ I enjoy being of service to others.

_____ I have a sense of harmony and inner peace.

_____ I have a sense of balance in my life.

_____ I feel a responsibility to preserve the environment.

_____ I see myself as a person of worth and feel comfortable with my own strengths and limitations.

TO THINK ABOUT: There are no right or wrong responses. This assessment can help you identify areas in which you may decide to do some spiritual growth work. Continue to practice your positive spiritual health habits, and look for ways in which you can grow spiritually.

SPIRITUAL WELLNESS WORKSHEET

What activities do you currently practice that help you feel spiritually healthy?

When all the surface layers of your life are peeled away, what do you believe makes up the core of your life; your purpose for being?

List two items from the Spiritual Wellness Assessment that you rated with an *S* and that you believe are most important for your spiritual well-being. Why are these items so important to you?

Of the items you rated *SS* or *NS*, which two do you think are most important for your spiritual growth?

What are some specific things that you could do to grow in the two areas listed above?

THE POWER OF PERCEPTIONS

> *Rejoice always, pray without ceasing, give thanks in all circumstances; for this is the will of God in Christ Jesus for you.*
>
> *(I Thessalonians 5:16-18)*

"The sky is falling! The sky is falling!"
—Chicken Little

*W*as the sky really falling? Of course not. Yet Chicken Little believed it was. This stressed little chicken felt all the fear and apprehension as if the sky really were falling. Our perception becomes our reality. What we expect or believe will happen is what we actually experience. We create our own reality. As Henry Ford said, "Whether you believe you can or believe you can't, either way you're right." If you wake up dreading the day ahead, full of stress, and just wanting to get it over with, then ask yourself this question, "Is my perception affecting my reality?"

This reminds me of a story a former nursing student, Jane Summer Edwards, told me about Martha. Martha was a mildly retarded but fairly well-functioning member of a group home where Jane worked. Martha was so accustomed to an institutionalized life in which she was always told what she had to get done, that she viewed *everything* as a task "to get over with." She would say things like, "I guess I'll have my coffee and dessert now and get it over with." Or, "I guess I'll go take my bath now and get it over with." It didn't matter that the bath was a leisurely bubble bath that she had all the time in the world to take—a luxury in the staff's eyes. The staff would laugh and say things like "I guess I'll go and see that movie tonight and get it over with," or "Might as well take my vacation time now and get it over with." Are there things in your life, like Martha's dessert or bubble bath, that you should find joyful rather than just something "to get over with?"

There is a story about two men sitting on their porch looking out at the evening. One sees the mud, the other sees the stars. Can you begin to focus more on the positive? Can seeing the blessings rather than the burdens bring less stress to you? Can you see the stars rather than the mud? Your perception of what happens to you may be the most important factor in the quality of your life!

I keep the following Persian proverb in my memory. It has put things in perspective to help me manage stress more than once!

> *I murmured because I had no shoes,*
> *Until I met a man who had no feet.*

Let me ask you once again, could seeing the blessings rather than the burdens bring less stress to you?

There is a story about the great diva, Beverly Sills. She had just given an outstanding matinee performance, and according to the program, she would give another performance that evening. Backstage she was being congratulated by one of her fans. He said, "You must rest now, because I see that you have to give another performance tonight." "No," said Beverly Sills. "I don't have to give another performance tonight." "Well," said the fan, "it says here in the program that you have an eight P.M. performance. Did you forget?" "I do have a performance tonight," she said, "but I don't *have* to give it. I *get* to give it." Her perception surely affected her reality.

I have to warn you, though, that in spite of your best efforts, you will have days when it is hard to see the positive. I wrote the following poem one day when my perception was seriously affecting my reality:

Stress, stress, oh what a mess
I must confess, I'd be happy with less
Yes it's true for success, one must have some stress
But I'd feel truly blessed, to be feeling less stressed.

Do you know the feeling? My point is that even with your best efforts, you will have days that feel out of control. Yet the way you choose to think about the events in your life will have a tremendous impact on the quality of your life.

Last year I got glasses. I was totally amazed at how clear and sharp the world around me became when I put on my glasses. Had the world around me changed? No. The difference was that I could now see the world clearly. I had become so accustomed to the dull and blurry view that I was not even aware of what I was missing. The world didn't change. I did. Can you learn to see things in your life differently? Yes, you can!

I heard a great example of this. A lady was visiting her elderly father-in-law. When they sat in the backyard and tried to visit she found the neighbor's loud music to be very irritating and was sure this would be stressful to her father-in-law. Finally, when her stress level had risen to the point that she had to say something, she said, "Dad, how can you stand your neighbor's loud music? That must be so annoying to you." The elderly gentleman replied, "Not at all. I'm just thankful I can still hear the music." The same event, yet two very different responses.

First, think of the events or people causing you stress. Next, be willing to open your mind to a new way of thinking about these things. Are you angry with anyone? Try pretending that you are the defense lawyer for that person. Your job is to make a case for his or her behavior. You might actually come to see the other side of the story and view the whole situation with much less stress. See the blessing instead of the burden.

Even when we cannot change the things that cause us stress, we can change our perception. Thomas Edison was perceiving things in a positive manner when he said, "I have not failed 10,000 times. I have successfully found 10,000 ways that will not work." Now that is a positive perception!

If you are feeling like Chicken Little and experiencing "the sky is falling" kind of stress in your life, then ask for God's help in changing your perception. Expect the day to be good. Expect to be in control of your thoughts and emotions. See the blessings that surround you. Take control by viewing yourself as a positive force, rather than as a passive person reacting by rote in a negative manner to stress-producing events.

Your perception is the key that unlocks the door to stress less living. Perception has the power to create or reduce stress. You have control over your perception, how you see things. It is your choice! How empowering it is to know that you can choose to see the events in your life in a more positive manner!

Think about Romans 12:2: "Do not be conformed to this world, but be transformed by the renewing of your minds, so that you may discern what is the will of God—what is good and acceptable and perfect."

Message to Remember

Your perception is the key that unlocks the door to stress less living. By choosing to view events from a positive perspective you can reduce the stress in your life and experience each day more abundantly. Life is not something "to get over with."

Start Today

Pick out one thing today that causes you stress. Think about the person, event, or experience from a fresh and positive perspective. Make a deliberate effort to put aside your old, stress-producing way of viewing this situation. Pray for God's guidance.

Sometime today make a list of things you love—people, places, smells, sounds. Be spontaneous—like brainstorming, do not try to make sense of the ideas that come to your mind, just allow the ideas to flow. Post your list in a place where you can see it often and add to it.

Pray for God's help to "set your minds on things that are above, not on things that are on earth..." (Colossians 3:2).

Evening Reflections

What was the stressful situation that you chose to view from a more positive perspective? Were you able to change your perspective? Think about the wonderful blessing you are giving yourself and those around you when you free yourself from a negative, stress-producing view. Consider the words of William Shakespeare, "Nothing is good or bad but thinking makes it so."

Did listing the things you love help you become more aware of the blessings that surround you every day?

Reflect on II Corinthians 4:15: "Yes, everything is for your sake, so that grace, as it extends to more and more people, may increase thanksgiving, to the glory of God."

Clear your mind for a few minutes and think about the impact that changing some of your perceptions would have on your life. What if each morning you thought of something or someone that is causing you stress, and you prayed for God's help to think of this situation in a new, more positive way? What if you even gave thanks for the positive insight from the stress? If each day you decided to see one stress-producing experience from a positive perspective, your life would be changed!

Section 1 Chapter 5

*C*HANGE

*Y*ou have heard it, too: The only person who likes change is a wet baby. Change is not easy. We cling to the familiar. We are caught on the treadmill of our own habits. Try this: Fold your arms across your chest. Now try folding them with the other arm on top. Next, fold your hands. Now fold them with the other thumb on top. Feels funny and unnatural doesn't it? You will fold your arms the same way every time *unless* you are consciously thinking about changing. You can do it the other way, but you have to be conscious and deliberate about it, just as you must be conscious and deliberate about choosing behaviors that will result in more peaceful living.

So, while it is true that change can be unsettling, change is the very thing that will help you grow and accomplish the things you desire in your life. You can have a more balanced and less stressed life if you make some changes.

Researchers have learned that people go through stages in the process of change. I have adapted these stages and applied them to a Christian perspective. The following is a brief explanation of the stages of change for Christians and an example of how they might relate to you as you change to a more stress-managed lifestyle.

Change Process

"I wish" stage—You are not even thinking about changing. I think of the poem we used to recite when I was a child: "Star light, star bright, first star I see tonight, I wish I may, I wish I might, have the wish I wish tonight." Of course we know that simply wishing on a star will not make our wishes come true. People in this stage of change say things like, "I wish I had more money so I wouldn't have to worry" or "I wish I wasn't feeling so overwhelmed all the time" or "If only Sam would stop drinking—he causes me so much stress." So in the "I wish" stage you are not seriously thinking about changing your behavior.

"I might" stage—You are beginning to think about changing. You might start weighing the advantages and disadvantages of making a change. This is where you hear "I think I need some help dealing with stress. I might look into some programs next month." You are not really committed at this point, but you are starting to see the need to change.

"I will" stage—You make small changes. You decide to read *Stress Less* or study the book in your small group at church. You start to learn about different stress reduction strategies. You see the importance of changing some behaviors. You begin to realize that God desires wholeness and healing in your life.

"I do" stage—You make bigger changes. This also can be called the **action** stage. You spend thirty minutes every day in prayer and meditation. You allow God to show you the underlying causes of stress in your life. You take action and you trust in God to care for you. "Not by might, nor by power, but by my spirit, says the LORD of hosts" (Zechariah 4:6).

"I believe" stage—You have incorporated the changes into your lifestyle. This **maintenance** stage is a critical step in the change process. Once you have identified the true source of your stress, then you are able to break out of the cycle. You know that anger, doubt, fear, and worry will be changed by the power of the Holy Spirit working in your life. Your daily quiet time of prayer, meditation, and surrender is part of your routine now. It's a habit.

The "oops" stage—You have relapsed. This is considered a stage of change because so many of us relapse to previous behavior. This is when Christmas comes, you have fifteen people at your home for the holidays, and your routine is totally non-existent. You do not even have time to brush your teeth, let alone pray and meditate.

Relapse may result in returning to any of the previous stages. Relapse happens—expect it. No need to beat yourself up with guilt. Just acknowledge that you have lapsed back to your old behaviors temporarily. Think about what you can learn from this relapse, then make a plan for starting your healthy behavior again as soon as possible.

Remind yourself that to walk in victory requires continual renewal of your heart and mind. Know that God will help you get back on track. Remember that life is a journey and the road to stress less living includes some detours and back-tracking. What is important is keeping your eyes focused on your destination.

In my work with health promotion I have seen the same pattern. An individual desires to make a lifestyle change (lose weight, stop smoking, exercise, manage stress). Things move along nicely until the action stage. This is where things get tricky. You have to *do* something to get the results you desire, and you have to *keep* doing it. Knowing is not enough. Starting is not enough.

Many of the people in my weight management classes are experts on weight loss. They know the facts. Their challenge is in translating the facts into behaviors that they can maintain for a lifetime. This reminds me of Mark Twain's remark, "Stopping smoking is easy. I've done it a hundred times." Or as Will Rogers once put it, "Even if you're on the right track, you'll get run over if you just sit there." You have to move. You must take action and maintain that action. Knowing that God loves you unconditionally is a powerful motivator for wanting to live your life in full accord with God's desires for you.

So take action now. You will learn how it feels to take control of your life.

Change is not easy; you might need some help along the way. Can you relate to this person's prayer for help?

Dear Lord,

So far today I've done all right. I haven't gossiped, haven't lost my temper, haven't been greedy, grumpy, nasty, selfish or overindulgent. But ... in a few minutes, God, I'm going to get out of the bed and from then on I'm probably going to need a lot more help. Thank you. Amen.

Message to Remember

Change will help you grow and accomplish what is important to you. Understand where you are in the change process. Call on God for help and guidance.

Start Today

A man once told me that on high stress days, he wears his watch on his right wrist instead of his left wrist where he normally wears it. Every time he checks the time he is reminded to slow down and relax.

My friend Larry told me, "When I come to a red (stop) light in traffic, I remind myself to stop, slow down and relax. When the light turns green (go), I thank God for my blessings. I do this, and it really helps me."

Try one of these ideas or change one thing about your daily routine today that will remind you to slow down and relax. Remember, thinking about it is not enough. The one thing I will do to change my routine today is . . .

Evening Reflections

Some people thrive on change while others prefer the routine and predictable. How about you?

What is the one most important change you could make in your life to reduce your stress? How can you begin?

Reflect on these verses from Paul's letter to the Philippians: "And this is my prayer, that your love may overflow more and more with knowledge and full insight to help you determine what is best, so that in the day of Christ you may be pure and blameless, having produced the harvest of righteousness that comes through Jesus Christ for the glory and praise of God" (Philippians 1: 9-11).

$\mathscr{L}$IVING IN THE PRESENT

So do not worry about tomorrow, for tomorrow will bring worries of its own. Today's trouble is enough for today. (Matthew 6:34)

$\mathscr{T}$he present moment is where life can be found, and if you don't arrive there, you miss your appointment with life. I once saw a bumper sticker that said, "Life is not a dress rehearsal." Today is not practice for some future performance. Today is life. If we spend much of our time and energy dwelling on the past and worrying about the future we miss the gift of the moment we have. There is a saying that goes, "Yesterday is history. Tomorrow is a mystery. Today is a gift, which is why we call it the present." Feel the peace that can come from enjoying the moment.

Take a minute or two to repeat this breathing activity. Breathing in say, "This is the day," and breathing out say, "That the Lord hath made." Put your book down, close your eyes, and enjoy the calm and peaceful feeling of being in the moment. No need to worry about tomorrow or think about yesterday. Just enjoy being alive at this moment.

Think about this short story:

There are two days in every week about which we should not worry, two days that should be kept free from fear and apprehension.

One of the two days is YESTERDAY, with its mistakes and cares, its faults and blunders, its aches and pains. Yesterday has passed forever beyond our control. All the money in the world cannot bring back yes-

terday. We cannot undo a single act we performed. We cannot erase a single word we said. Yesterday is gone.

The other day we should not worry about is TOMORROW, with its possible adversities, its burdens, its large promise and poor performance. Tomorrow is also beyond our immediate control. Tomorrow's sun will rise, either in splendor or behind a mask of clouds—but it will rise. Until it does, we have no stake in tomorrow, for it is yet unborn.

This leaves only one day—TODAY. Anyone can fight the battles of just one day. It is only when you and I add the burdens of those two awful eternities—yesterday and tomorrow—that we break down.

It is not the experience of today that drives us mad—it is remorse or bitterness for something that happened yesterday and the dread of what tomorrow may bring. Let us, therefore, live but one day at a time.

Source unknown

A friend jokingly told me that maybe instead of calling ourselves human beings we more appropriately could be called human doings. Her point was that we are so busy always *doing* that we forget to just *be*. Just to be present in the moment is a powerful stress reducer. I have heard this called mindfulness. It is a modern-day form of an ancient Asian technique that involves maintaining awareness in the present moment. The idea is that you tune in to yourself. You allow whatever you experience, a sensation, a smell, a thought, a sound to enter your awareness. Mindfulness helps keep you in the present, thinking about *what is* rather than about *what if* or *if only*.

Even our daily work, which at times can feel like drudgery, can take on a stress-relieving feeling if we view the moment as part of our contribution to bigger priorities. Thinking about today, this minute, the task at hand in a positive manner brings a feeling of peace and contentment. There is the old story about two people laying bricks. One says to the other, "What are you doing?" The other one answers, "Laying bricks. What are you doing?" The first one responds, "Building a cathedral."

We have opportunities every day to be mindful. Yet in our haste to do more and do it faster we miss the moment. Have you become a master of doing more than one thing at a time? You know what I mean—putting on your makeup and filing your fingernails as you drive to work; making your bed while you brush your teeth; reading the paper while your daughter is talking to you. I am all for using time efficiently, but you may be missing many pleasurable moments. Mindfulness is freeing, relaxing, and nurturing.

Your spirit and mind cannot be open to God's desires, love, and grace when you are consumed with past failures or future worries. Let the healing power of the Creator free you from the pain of the past. Let today be a new story of victory and hope in your life.

Message to Remember

Experience mindfulness. That is, be conscious and deliberate about appreciating and enjoying this moment, this day. These moments and days are your life.

Start Today

At least twice today, when you are beginning to feel the pressure build, be deliberate in clearing your mind of all distraction and simply enjoy the moment. Think of the sights, sounds, and smells that surround you at that moment. Breathing in say, "This is the day," and breathing out say, "That the Lord hath made." Be thankful for the present.

Evening Reflections

Reflect back on a typical day. What past and future worries keep replaying in your mind? Clear these thoughts from your mind to allow more time for enjoying the present. Do you miss the experience of the present by filling your mind with what needs to be done in the future or what already has happened in the past?

What can you do to remind yourself to be conscious and deliberate about enjoying the moment?

Write a prayer of thanksgiving for the blessings in your life today.

"Do not remember the former things, / or consider the things of old. / I am about to do a new thing; / now it springs forth, do you not perceive it?" (Isaiah 43:18-19).

*C*LEAR THE CLUTTER

Let us know, let us press on to know the LORD*; | his appearing is as sure as the dawn; | he will come to us like the showers, | like the spring rains that water the earth. (Hosea 6:3)*

---

*W*e know deep down that life is about more than having the latest fashions, the best toys, the newest car, the biggest house. We can make choices that enable us to gain control of our lives, and we can refuse to allow these things to dictate where our time and money goes. We can remove things from our lives that are not really important. We can learn to live simply.

Think about this story and how it relates to your life. A lone fisherman sat on the beach. His fishing pole was planted in the sand. Along came a businessman on vacation. "Why don't you have two poles so you can catch more fish?" the businessman asked. "Then what would I do?" asked the fisherman. "Then you could take the extra money, buy a boat, get nets and a crew, and catch even more fish." "Then what would I do?" asked the fisherman. "Then," said the businessman, "you could move up to a fleet of large ships, go wholesale, and become very rich." "Then what would I do?" asked the fisherman. "Then you could do whatever you want!" shouted the businessman. And the fisherman replied, "I am."

I watched a TV show recently that talked about a growing epidemic of "affluenza" in America. They were talking about the disease-like condition of affluence—having to have more and more material possessions. Part of the disease is the belief that this stuff will somehow make us happy. I am reminded of the story about a millionaire who was asked, "How much money would it take to make you content?" He replied, "Just a little bit more." It is the never ending desire to acquire.

This ongoing battle with consumerism can lead us to a dangerous trap—spending beyond our means. The more we make the more we spend. The cycle never ends as we want more, more, more. We confuse the have-to-have's with the want-to-have's. As with the millionaire, we always want just a little bit more. The more you have the more you have to take care of, to insure, to maintain. It is like running on a treadmill where you have to run faster and faster just to stay in the same place. Stress!

Think about your life. Can you resist the temptation to continually raise your standard of living? Is this what you really want? What will bring you peace and happiness? Do you sometimes feel lost in the rush to succeed? Do you lose focus of the joy that life can hold? Take time to think about how you are living your life, and realize that contentment comes from within. Ultimately knowing God and God's love for you will help you make choices to reduce your stress. As with any problem, awareness is the first step toward resolution. If you allow the world around you to become the yardstick by which you measure happiness, you may have a case of affluenza.

My routine the last couple of years has been to read the morning paper while I eat breakfast. The problem is that it takes me about half an hour to read the paper and I often felt rushed to get ready for the day. In an effort to simplify my life, I decided to stop reading the morning paper and instead take fifteen minutes for prayer and meditation. The benefits were immediate and I plan to make this a lifelong habit. I start the day more relaxed and prepared to deal with what comes. I have more time to touch base with my family. I use the money I spent on the paper for a mission project our church supports. It is truly a winning choice for me. This one small change to simplify my life has made a difference.

The key to contentment is keeping things in the proper perspective. You can simplify your life by understanding that material things will not necessarily make you happy. Strive to live your life based on a close relationship with God and you will find the path to inner contentment. You deserve a peaceful and happy life. By simplifying your life and living within your means, you will discover inner peace.

Message to Remember
Clear the clutter from your life. Inner peace and contentment come from within and from the Savior.

Start Today
Do one realistic and specific thing to simplify your life today.

Evening Reflection
Meditate on I Timothy 6: 6-11: "Of course, there is great gain in godliness combined with contentment; for we brought nothing into the world, so that we can take nothing out of it; but if we have food and clothing, we will be content with these. But those who want to be rich fall into temptation and are trapped by many senseless and harmful desires that plunge people into ruin and destruction. For the love of money is a root of all kinds of evil, and in their eagerness to be rich some have wandered away from the faith and pierced themselves with many pains. But as for you, man of God, shun all this; pursue righteousness, godliness, faith, love, endurance, gentleness."

The focus of the seven chapters in section one is on getting started. You learned about
- The importance of caring for yourself
- Using Psalm 23 to restore your soul
- Balance and a strong spiritual foundation
- The power of your perceptions in shaping your reality
- The process of change
- Enjoying the moment—*this is your life*
- Clearing the clutter for inner contentment

What is the single most important thing you have learned from the seven chapters in section one?

⁘SSESSING YOUR STRESS

...but those who wait for the LORD *shall renew their strength, / they shall mount up with wings like eagles, / they shall run and not be weary, they shall walk and not faint. (Isaiah 40:31)*

---

tress, stressors, eustress, distress, good stress, bad stress—it can be pretty confusing and downright stressful to understand what stress is all about. As Hans Selye, the noted stress researcher, once said, "Stress is a scientific concept which has suffered from the mixed blessing of being too well known and too little understood."

Stress-related problems are on the rise. The American Academy of Family Physicians estimates that symptoms linked to stress account for about two-thirds of all visits to family physicians. In the seven chapters of section two we will look at the nature of stress. You will explore the causes of stress in your life and learn about the effects of stress on your body, mind, and spirit. Your reaction to stressors can be divided into two broad categories: psychological (mind) and physiological (body). Recognizing stress and then coping with it successfully are processes you can learn.

Stress has been called the modern-day plague, an out of control epidemic. According to *Prevention Magazine*'s 1996 annual Prevention Index Survey, nearly three-quarters of adults (73 percent) say they feel great stress on a weekly basis. In 1983, only 55 percent of Index respondents had the same response. The problem is growing. Talk to school children, college students, baby boomers, and retired folks; you will hear the same messages: Too much to do, constant pressure, my life feels out of control, no time for myself.

Timelock

The term *timelock* describes a condition when demands on our time become so overwhelming that it feels impossible to squeeze one more second out of our packed schedule. You simply feel you just cannot do one more thing. At times like this you may throw your hands in the air and give up.

Telltale symptoms of timelock include:
- Rushing
- Chronic difficulty with making decisions and choices
- Fatigue
- Feeling overwhelmed
- Frequently missed deadlines
- Not enough time for rest, relationships, and renewal

There are plenty of things to cause you stress. Money, kids, jobs, in-laws, relationships, home responsibilities, retirement, even trying to stay healthy can cause you stress. I wrote this little poem called "I Think I'll Just Go Take a Snooze" about the stress we may feel from all the shoulds and ought-tos we face each day.

I Think I'll Just Go Take a Snooze
By Margie Hesson

Get your vitamin E and your vitamin C
*   and calcium for osteoporosis.*
Trying to get all the right things to eat
*   could cause you a case of neurosis.*

Roughage, fiber, bulk, and bran
*   If you wanna prevent constipation.*
Eat your beans and munch on prunes,
*   talk about a bloated sensation.*

Then you brush and you floss and you gargle a lot

to prevent that dreaded halitosis.
You gotta take care of your pearly whites
or end up with a toothless diagnosis.

Don't forget exercise—are you getting enough?
Is your pulse in the target zone?
A leisurely stroll just won't do anymore
for maximal muscle tone.

Take time to listen and be a good friend
and don't forget to journal.
The list of things you ought to do
can sometimes seem eternal.

Stay out of the sun, lay off the caffeine
staying healthy just isn't that easy.
Have a pap, check for lumps, get a physical too
my pressure's rising, I feel rather queasy.

There's miles to jog and muscles to stretch
and as always those pounds to lose.
To tell you the truth, I feel rather stressed
I think I'll just go take a snooze.

OK, I admit it; I am poking fun here. All of these things are important, but my intent is to help diffuse some of the tension of feeling overwhelmed. There is so much to do, sometimes it is easier to just do nothing—to go take a snooze.

Complete the Ardell Wellness Stress Test at the end of this chapter to help you identify some of the stressors in your life. Identifying the sources of your stress is the important first step in managing your stress.

There is not one best tool for assessing stress, in part because reactions to events vary from person to person. What frazzles one person may excite or challenge another. Research increasingly supports the idea that it is not the amount of stress that matters, but one's ability to control the situations that contribute to it. Often, external events do not cause stress; how we perceive and cope with them does. So use this test (and others) to give you an indication of the stress in your life, but do not rely on the findings completely.

Message to Remember

Understanding the causes of stress is an important first step to managing stress in your life.

Start Today

Complete the Ardell Wellness Stress Test following this chapter. Think carefully about the causes of stress in your life.

Evening Reflections

Look back over your stress assessment. What did you learn from your results? Were you surprised by what you learned? Are there other causes of stress that were not included on this stress assessment?

Read and meditate on Psalm 94:18-19: "When I thought, 'My foot is slipping,' / your steadfast love, O LORD, held me up. / When the cares of my heart are many, / your consolations cheer my soul."

The Ardell Wellness Stress Test

Rate your satisfaction with each of the following areas by using the following scale:

+3=ecstatic   +2=very happy   +1=mildly happy   0=indifferent
-1=mildly disapproving -2=very disapproving -3=completely dismayed

_____ 1. Choice of career
_____ 2. Present job/business
_____ 3. Marital status
_____ 4. Primary relationships
_____ 5. Capacity to have fun
_____ 6. Amount of fun experienced in last month
_____ 7. Financial prospects
_____ 8. Current income level
_____ 9. Spirituality
_____ 10. Level of self-esteem
_____ 11. Prospects for having impact on those who know you and possibly others
_____ 12. Sex life
_____ 13. Body, how it looks and performs
_____ 14. Home life
_____ 15. Life skills and knowledge of issues and facts unrelated to your job or profession
_____ 16. Learned stress management capacities
_____ 17. Nutritional knowledge, attitudes, and choices
_____ 18. Ability to recover from disappointment, hurts, setbacks, and tragedies
_____ 19. Confidence that you are now at or will in the future come reasonably close to your highest potential
_____ 20. Achievement of a rounded or balanced quality in your life
_____ 21. Sense that life for you is on an upward curve, getting better and fuller all the time
_____ 22. Level of participation in issues and concerns beyond your immediate interests
_____ 23. Choice whether to parent or not and with the consequences or results of that choice
_____ 24. Role in some kind of network of friends, relatives, and/or others about whom you care deeply and who reciprocate that commitment to you
_____ 25. Emotional acceptance of the inescapable reality of aging

                                                    TOTAL_____

The Ardell Wellness Stress Test Interpretation

+51 to +75   This is a self-actualized person, nearly immune from the ravages of stress. There are few if any challenges likely to untrack him or her from a sense of near total well-being.

+25 to +50   This person has mastered the wellness approach to life and has the capacity to deal creatively and efficiently with events and circumstances.

+1 to +24   This is a wellness-oriented person, with an ability to prosper as a whole person, but he or she should give a bit more attention to optimal health concepts and skill building.

0 to –24   This is a candidate for additional training in how to deal with stress. A sudden increase in potentially negative events and circumstances could cause a severe emotional setback.

–25 to –50   This person is a candidate for counseling. He or she is either too pessimistic or has severe problems in dealing with stress.

–51 to –75   This is a candidate for major psychological care with virtually no capacity for coping with life's problems.

(From *High Level Wellness: An Alternative to Doc, Drugs and Disease* by Don Ardell. Used by permission.)

$\mathscr{S}$TRESS: WHAT IS IT?

Those of steadfast mind you keep in peace— / in peace because they trust in you. (Isaiah 26:3)

$\mathscr{S}$tress is a very interesting phenomenon. You may feel that you can't live with it, and you can't live without it. We are surrounded by stress everyday. Some people thrive on stress and find it to be the stimulus for growth and higher achievement. For others, stress is overwhelming and debilitating. So what is stress?

We commonly use the word *stress* to refer to both the effects of stress and to stressors, the events or conditions that produce stress. You might think of stress as being both your boss (the stressor) and the effect he or she has on your body (headache, muscle tension, indigestion). It might be helpful to think of *stressors* as the situations that trigger physical and emotional reactions and the term *stress response* as those reactions.

Stress may be viewed as an absence of inner peace, a loss of control, or any change experienced by an individual. Hans Selye researched the physical aspects of stress. He defined stress as the nonspecific response of the body to any demand placed upon it to adapt, whether the demand produces pleasure or pain. Many experts believe that your physical reaction to stress is the same whether you are feeling positive or negative stress. So even something positive such as a vacation or a promotion at work can cause the same physical stress response in your body as a negative event such as getting a traffic ticket or being demoted at work.

Richard Lazarus, in the late 1960s, proposed a new idea that stress is a relationship between the person and the environment that the person perceives as taxing or exceeding his or her resources and endangering his or her well-being. The work of Lazarus is very important because *perception* is considered the key to the experience of stress.

I find it useful to think of stress as the perception that events or circumstances challenge or exceed a person's ability to cope. These events may be real or imagined threats to one's mental, physical, emotional, or spiritual well-being that result in a series of physiological responses and adaptations. Perception is the important concept here. It explains why one person will feel absolutely overwhelmed and helpless in a situation while another person in that same situation feels exhilarated.

For example, Rich and Angie are students in my class. I announced in class that this semester, rather than write a paper, each student would give an oral presentation in class. Rich was absolutely terrified at the idea of talking in front of his peers while Angie was excited about not having to write a paper and stimulated by the idea of making a presention in class. The same assignment, yet two very different responses.

The bottom line is that stress is a rather complex phenomenon involving body, mind, and spirit. The many factors affecting stress are not fully understood. We know that stress is more than physiological arousal; the body is affected by the games of the mind. Remember, the way you perceive a stressor determines how that stressor affects your body.

You have probably heard the terms "good stress" or eustress and "bad stress" or distress. We need a certain amount of good stress to help us function and be productive. This eustress adds a positive, enhancing dimension to the quality of life. Distress, frequently abbreviated to simply *stress*, diminishes the quality of life.

These three things are important to remember about stress:
1. Stress results in physiological changes to your body.
2. Your perception determines how stress affects you.
3. You can learn to manage stress.

Message to Remember

Stress results from the perception that certain events, people, and conditions challenge our ability to cope. Your perception of stressors affects your body's physical response.

Start Today

Begin your day by reading and meditating on Philippians 4:13: "I can do all things through him who strengthens me."

For the next few days, keep a stress journal. Imagine that you are strolling beside yourself observing the person you have become and the habits you have developed. Health Educator Dr. Larry Tentinger suggests addressing these three questions:

What? What was the stress producing behavior? Record the time, place and circumstances. What were you doing, thinking, or feeling?

So what? So how did this behavior make you feel?

Now what? Now what can you do differently to avoid the stress-producing outcome?

This is an extremely valuable activity because it forces you to be aware of the specific events, people, or conditions that push your buttons. Write the answers to these questions as soon as possible after you have experienced a stress response. This may happen several times a day.

Evening Reflections

Look back over your stress journal. Do you see any patterns?

Think about the idea that not only do you receive stress, you also give stress or contribute to the stress of others. Reflect on ways that you might be adding to the stress of others. Consider things like impatient driving, loud noise, and argumentative or intolerant behavior toward others. Think of two people who you suspect experience added stress because of you. Write down how you cause these people stress and one thing you can do to lessen their stress. Pray for God's guidance.

Clear your mind, relax, and once again read Psalm 23.

Section 2 Chapter 10

$\mathcal{B}$USY BODY—
PHYSICAL RESPONSES TO STRESSORS

Peace I leave with you; my peace I give to you. I do not give to you as the world gives. Do not let your hearts be troubled, and do not let them be afraid. (John 14:27)

$\mathcal{E}$very minute of every day your body is busy doing its work. Cells are continually dying and being replaced, oxygen is delivered to faraway corners of your body, bones are being built, food is being turned into energy, and so it goes—moment by moment, hour by hour, day by day, year by year. When all is well, you seldom notice what is going on inside your body.

What happens inside your body in response to stress? The physiological response to stressors is remarkably similar in our bodies. Physically everyone responds to stress in basically the same predictable way. When you are out for a walk and a very large barking and growling dog jumps out at you from behind a house, your body will respond in a very predictable manner. You will begin to perspire, your heart rate will increase, your muscles will tense, your throat will become dry, and you may feel nauseated. You know the feeling. This typical physical response has been described by Hans Selye as the General Adaptation Syndrome (GAS).

General Adaptation Syndrome

The body progresses through the following three stages when confronted by stressors:

1. **Alarm Reaction Stage**—This is sometimes called the fight-or-flight reaction. Your body reacts to a threat by preparing for physical action. Responses include dilating the bronchi to allow more air into the lungs, accelerating the heart rate to pump oxygen throughout the body, releasing extra sugar from the liver into the blood to provide an energy boost, tensing of muscles in preparation for action, releasing endorphins to relieve pain in case of injury, and increasing perspiration to cool the skin.

2. **Resistance Stage**—The body readjusts, returning to normal functioning as stress symptoms diminish. Our bodies strive for a balanced state called homeostasis in which our heart rate, blood pressure, hormone level, breathing, and other vital functions are maintained in a normal range. Following a stressful event, the parasympathetic nervous system kicks in to restore homeostasis and calm your body. This resistance phase is very important because it allows you to recover from stressors and get on with the regular work that your body does such as digestion, muscle building, and cell repair. You can then get on with your life.

3. **Exhaustion Stage**—What happens, though, if you find yourself confronted with a series of stressors or a stressor that persists for a long time? If the stressful situation does not end and the alarm reaction continues for a long time, the body's ability to adjust diminishes. If the body's reserves of adaptive energy are spent, the result is general exhaustion. This is not the kind of exhaustion you feel from being tired after a long day's work. This is the kind of physiological exhaustion that can be life-threatening. Your adaptive energy stores are depleted and serious illness may result.

Fight-or-Flight

Fight-or-flight, what is it? During the alarm stage of the General Adaptation Syndrome, our body gears up for action to deal with a stressor. Harvard physiologist Walter Cannon named this physiological reaction to a threat the fight-or-flight response. This reaction is part of our biological heritage and has served humankind well as a survival mechanism.

A common example is the caveman who is sitting peacefully by his fire when suddenly a large bear jumps out of the forest.

The caveman's fight-or-flight response is critical for his survival. He must either fight the bear or take flight—run like crazy to get out of there. In either case, his body must enter a state of physical readiness. His heart rate increases to pump blood to vital organs, his muscles tense for action, his breathing increases to supply oxygen, his blood pressure rises to pump blood to working muscles, his liver excretes extra sugar to provide energy for his muscles and brain, muscles in his intestines and bladder relax to allow more blood flow to working organs. This is truly a life-saving and miraculous response to the physical threat of the bear type. This is what we call acute stress; it surfaces quickly, is usually intense, and dissipates quickly.

Following this brief time of physical readiness, the body strives to return to a more normal state. This happens during the resistance stage of the GAS when the parasympathetic nervous system takes over to calm your body.

The problem is that many of today's stressors are not the acute bear-type. In modern life, this is an antiquated mechanism that has not kept up with the development of the human mind. Think back to your stress assessment. How many of your stressors demanded this kind of response? Many of our stressors today are of the chronic nature that may not seem so intense but can go on for days, months, or years. In the next chapter we will explore some of these chronic stressors.

Message to Remember

The physical response of your body to stressors occurs in a predictable manner.

Start Today

Complete the "Are You Stressed Out?" test on the next page. This test, used in the Framingham Heart Study, can provide a rough gauge of how much stress you experience.

Answer yes or no:

Are You Stressed Out?

_____Are you often troubled by feelings of tenseness, restlessness, or inability to relax?

_____Are you often bothered by nervousness or shaking?

_____Do you have trouble sleeping or falling asleep?

_____Do you feel that you are under a great deal of tension?

_____Do you often have trouble relaxing?

_____Do you often have periods of restlessness so that you cannot sit for long?

_____Do you often feel that difficulties are piling up and are too much for you to handle?

The more times you answer yes, the greater your probable level of stress, and the more you will benefit from stress-reduction techniques. The exact relationship between these test scores and the risk of hypertension is not clear for all age groups. But for middle-aged working men and women, studies have shown that answering yes to at least five questions more than doubles the chance of developing high blood pressure.

Too much stress can contribute to physical changes such as hypertension. Do you know your blood pressure? If not, have it checked. Take your pulse when you are resting quietly, then again when you are feeling stressed. When you are stressed your body releases chemicals that cause your heart to beat faster. Your heart is like a pump that can wear out from working too hard. Think about the truly miraculous work your heart does. Be thankful.

Evening Reflections

Think back to an acute stressor that you experienced, such as a car pulling out in front of you or seeing your young child running after a ball into heavy traffic. You will know the feeling of the instantaneous response of your body. How did you feel? Thank God that our amazing bodies can respond in time of need.

Before you close your eyes to sleep tonight, think for a minute about the work of your body that continues through the night. This gift of life that you have been given is not to be taken for granted. It is a miracle.

CHRONIC STRESS AND ANGER

Whoever is slow to anger has great understanding, / but one who has a hasty temper exalts folly. / A tranquil mind gives life to the flesh...
(Proverbs 14:29-30)

Today we will explore the impact of chronic stress on your well-being with a focus on anger, possibly the most powerful stress emotion.

You learned in the previous chapter that your body is better suited for dealing with acute-type stress. Yet in modern-day life many of your stressors are more of the long-term or chronic type. Chronic stress can be deadly through its impact on your endocrine and immune systems. The ever growing credit card bill, a relationship that seems bad to stay in but worse to leave, feeling trapped in an unrewarding job, holding a grudge against someone who has hurt you, preoccupation with problems from your past, and a general feeling that your life is out of control can bring a sense of helplessness, hopelessness, and defeat. Chronic stress is the real bad guy in terms of your health. When your body stays in a continually aroused, stressed state, exhaustion and disease are inevitable.

So, ironically, the stresses and strains of our modern life have transformed a life-saving mechanism into a potentially life-threatening one. It is like continually gunning the engine on your car; your body stays keyed up, your engine wears out, and you eventually run out of gas. You do not relax and recharge. Many experts believe it is this continued elevated biochemical response that causes the physical changes leading to stress-related diseases such as immune dysfunction and heart disease.

When daily hassles, such as a slow driver in the fast lane or misplacing your keys, trigger the fight-or-flight response, it is only a matter of time before your health suffers. Indigestion and insomnia become chronic; arteries become rough, hard and clogged; and your heart strains under the load.

Recent research from the heart rehabilitation clinic of James Blumenthal at Duke University indicates that individuals who are high responders may be more at risk for heart problems. These people experience almost any negative emotion more intensely than other people. These emotions may include anger and hostility, but also less overtly stressful emotions such as fear, disappointment, and anxiety.

The stress emotion anger, if unresolved, can lead to burnout. Learning to manage anger is vital to controlling the chronic stress in your life.

Anger

"You must understand this, my beloved: let everyone be quick to listen, slow to speak, slow to anger; for your anger does not produce God's righteousness" (James 1: 19-20).

Possibly one of the greatest gifts you could give yourself would be to forgive someone toward whom you feel anger. Anger and hostility are negative emotions that have a powerful impact on your well-being. "For he is our peace; in his flesh he has made both groups into one and has broken down the dividing wall, that is, the hostility between us" (Ephesians 2:14).

In the early 70's studies identified two stress-related personality types: Type A and Type B. Type A personalities were competitive, driven, impatient, angry, time urgent, and perfectionistic. The thinking was that people with Type A personalities were more prone to heart attacks than the laid back, noncompetitive Type B personalities.

Experts today generally agree that there is more to understand before we can categorize people by these personality traits and predict their health outcome. Recent research indicates that it is not the hurry syndrome associated with Type A behavior that makes us sick. Instead, they have identified the most important, even dangerous, component of Type A behavior is anger and hostility.

Anger is one of the most powerful and, many feel, most uncomfortable emotions that we humans experience. Sometimes anger is directed at another person. You all know the story about Cain killing his brother Abel in a fit of jealous rage. At other times, the source of our anger can not be readily identified. This free-floating hostility can be especially insidious. You may know someone or you yourself may be a person who feels angry at the world, at life, at the cards you have been dealt.

Deal with your anger. Some of the stress-relieving strategies you will read about in section three will help. If anger is a serious problem for you, seek professional help in dealing with this negative emotion.

Here are a few tips for dealing with anger:
- **Assess your anger style**—Do you tend to hold your anger in or do you explode when you're angry?
- **Keep an anger diary**—Keep track of the events or conditions that trigger your anger and record how you react. Look for patterns and circumstances that lead to your boiling point. Use this information to head off anger-producing situations.
- **Learn ways to deal with anger**—Take time out; develop a support system; learn how to think in a new, more positive way about the things that make you angry; learn to talk about the feelings that precede your anger.

As humans, we are blessed with the ability to feel and to express the full range of emotions. For a less stressed and more abundant life, learn to control these emotions, not be controlled by them.

In the next chapter we look at some of the physical consequences of chronic stress.

Message to Remember

Chronic stress, if not managed in a healthy manner, will result in physiological exhaustion. Uncontrolled anger is a major source of chronic stress.

Start Today

Think of one person toward whom you feel anger. If you are angry with someone ask God to give you the strength to forgive that person. Write a letter explaining your desire to let go of your anger, and pray for the healing of the relationship.

Evening Reflections

Look back over your stress journal. Do you notice any patterns? Do you see opportunities to avoid situations that cause you stress or anger? Do you see new ways of thinking about these stressful events? Look especially at your "Now, what?" answers. If journaling has been a good experience for you, consider continuing.

Think about a typical day. Does your work or daily routine provide you with opportunities for activity and movement? Exercise helps reduce the build-up of tension that can result from too much stress. Do you think the amount of active time has decreased from your parents' generation to yours?

Once again read Psalm 23. Focus on the idea of restoring your body and soul. Think about getting a second chance, a new start, in making health promoting changes in your life.

Section 2 Chapter 12

$\mathscr{S}$TRESS: THE INSIDE STORY

...hungry and thirsty, / their soul fainted within them. / Then they cried to the Lord in their trouble, / and he delivered them from their distress; / he led them by a straight way, / until they reached an inhabited town. / Let them thank the Lord for his steadfast love, / for his wonderful works to humankind. / For he satisfies the thirsty, / and the hungry he fills with good things. (Psalm 107:5-9)

$\mathscr{A}$re you suffering from stress overload? How do you know when you are under too much stress? What are the early warning signals to watch for so you can prevent stress from adversely affecting your health? What is the physical toll of repeated stress on your body?

One of my students told me about the day she knew she needed help in dealing with stress. It was the day she got mad at her stove. It may sound like a laughing matter, but to Janet, there was nothing funny about it. Here is her story:

I had been having a hard time with the death of a close family member, school was not going as planned, and my kids were driving me nuts. I was storming around the kitchen, trying to get supper on the table, when my stove refused to work. It was like the last straw at that moment and I began yelling and screaming at the stove. I even threw my hot pads at it! I turned around to see my children staring at me in disbelief. They had never seen their mommy act like this before. When I saw the tears well up and spill over in my young son's eyes, I knew I had to find a better way to react to stress in my life. I started to take time for myself. I give myself a half hour for a walk and daily quiet time. This has helped me put things in perspective and it's good for my health as a bonus. My son has even told me, "Go for a walk, Mommy, and don't come back till you're happy."

I suspect every one of you can relate to Janet's story. Most of us have experienced an out of control reaction to too much stress. Let us look at some of the signals of stress overload. It is interesting that there is a wide variety of responses to too much stress. While one person might overeat, another might have no appetite at all. While one might become withdrawn and quiet, another might become hyperactive and overly involved. There are some typical signals, however, that can help alert you to stress overload. Watch for:

- overreacting to minor problems
- inappropriate anger or impatience
- increased use of tobacco, alcohol, or drugs
- feeling unable to relax
- difficulty in making decisions
- difficulty sleeping
- poor work performance
- overwhelming urge to cry or run and hide

Stress overload may also manifest itself in physical symptoms such as headaches, indigestion, neck and back aches, nausea, cold hands and feet, diarrhea or constipation, teeth grinding, shortness of breath, heart palpitations, muscle spasms, and skin problems. Of course, the list goes on and on. The bottom line is that too much stress clearly results in some physical changes in your mind and your body.

Most research indicates that while stress may not cause disease outright, it clearly makes you more susceptible to disease and illness. Researchers are only just beginning to unlock the complex web of physical and emotional interactions that eventually cause the body to break down. Let's look briefly at what repeated stress does to your body.

Immune System Effects
Suppression of the body's immune response may be one of

the most crucial results of stress. Studies have shown, for example, that during stressful test times, antibody levels in students were found to be lower than normal, indicating a greater vulnerability to infection.

Cardiovascular Effects

Many studies have found a strong connection between heart disease and stress. In the alarm phase of the stress response, heart rate increases and blood vessels constrict, causing blood pressure to rise. This can lead to atherosclerosis, heart attacks, and stroke. Research suggests that certain stress-related emotional responses increase the risk of heart disease. People who react to situations with anger and hostility, or who are cynical and mistrustful, are more likely to have heart attacks than people with more trusting personalities.

Other Distress Effects

Gastrointestinal—diarrhea, constipation, ulcers, irritable bowel syndrome, colitis

Skin disorders—dryness, itching, hives, acne

Nervous system—depression, insomnia, anxiety

Tension and migraine headaches

Dysfunctional relationships

Increased proneness to accidents

Sexual and reproductive problems

Backaches

Temporomandibular joint (TMJ) syndrome

The list goes on, and it appears that we will see even more health consequences from stress as the research continues. The research on the relationship between stress and cancer is especially interesting. Another area of research to watch is the field of psychoneuroimmunology—the study of the interaction between the brain and the immune system.

It is important to understand the negative consequences of stress, if for no other reason than to motivate you to take control of your stress. Reading the list of stress effects provides a powerful incentive to prevent these negative effects in your body.

Our focus in this chapter has been on the negative physical consequences of too much stress. There are also some important psychological responses to stress overload—fear, anxiety, anger, and worry to name a few. In the next chapter we will look at worry in more detail. Worry can have a profound impact on the quality of your life.

Message to Remember

There is a direct relationship between stress overload and illness. Evidence continues to mount that stress is a crucial factor in physical and emotional health.

Start Today

Prepare your mind and spirit to help you deal with the physical effects of stress. Do this today by reading Psalm 118:24: "This is the day that the LORD has made; / let us rejoice and be glad in it." Begin your day with rejoicing. Anytime today you begin to feel your stress level rising, pause and recite in your mind this scripture reading. I cannot help but smile to think what the response would be if you recited Psalm 118:24 out loud the next time you were in a situation in which tension was mounting.

Evening Reflections

What signals alert you to stress overload?

Do you experience any of the negative effects of stress described in this chapter?

If you started your day with Psalm 118:24, how did an attitude of praise affect you and your stress level? How did it affect your physical body? Could you tell a difference between today and other days when you began the day not quite so thankfully?

Thank God tonight for the promise in Lamentations 3:22-23: "The steadfast love of the LORD never ceases, / his mercies never come to an end; / they are new every morning; / great is your faithfulness."

Consider that each new day can be joyful; you can feel energized, uplifted, and full of vigor and strength when you begin with an attitude of praise and rejoicing.

WORRY

Therefore I tell you, do not worry about your life, what you will eat or what you will drink, or about your body, what you will wear. Is not life more than food, and the body more than clothing? Look at the birds of the air; they neither sow nor reap nor gather into barns, and yet your heavenly Father feeds them. Are you not of more value than they? And can any of you by worrying add a single hour to your span of life? And why do you worry about clothing? Consider the lilies of the field, how they grow; they neither toil nor spin, yet I tell you, even Solomon in all his glory was not clothed like one of these. But if God so clothes the grass of the field, which is alive today and tomorrow is thrown into the oven, will he not much more clothe you—you of little faith? Therefore do not worry, saying, "What will we eat?" or "What will we drink?" or "What will we wear?" For it is the Gentiles who strive for all these things, and indeed your heavenly Father knows that you need all these things. But strive first for the kingdom of God and his righteousness, and all these things will be given to you as well. (Matthew 6:25-33)

I come from a family of worriers. My grandma worried, my mom worries, and I worry. It's kind of like it's our job to worry about the people we love. Of course, I know on an intellectual level that worry does no good. This scripture reading raises the question, "Can any of you by worrying add a single hour to your span of life?" We all know the answer to that question. Still, it is a hard habit to break. Especially, I tell myself, since it is in my genes.

One day I made a list of things I love. I was writing down things spontaneously and there on the list, along with buckskin horses and Chee-tos, was "I love the sound of the garage door going up." What a peculiar thing to love—until I gave it some thought. When our children Jenny and David were younger, I would worry every time they drove the car. The sound of the garage door going up was my cue that they were home safely once again. Oh, what a lovely sound! I could stop worrying.

A woman recently told me she thinks of worry as a sin. That sounded pretty harsh to me at the time, but I have given it a lot of thought since then, and she may be right. If you believe the message of today's scripture, then you can trust God to care for you. The part about you of little faith jumps out at me here. Scripture tells us that "faith is the assurance of things hoped for, the conviction of things not seen" (Hebrews 11:1). When we bathe in the assurance of God's love we are washed clean from worry.

A friend told me that he used to bring worries home from work. He knew this had a negative impact on the quality of his home life. Here is what Ken told me:

We have a bush right by our driveway. I designated that bush as "Ken's worry bush." Now, when I pull in the driveway at the end of the day, I dump my work worries at the bush. I mentally leave them there to be picked up in the morning when I return to work. This simple mental activity has really helped me.

I tried Ken's idea and use it to help clear my mind when I walk along beautiful Spearfish Creek. I realized that on some of my walks I spent the entire time worrying about things. So sometimes I mentally imagine throwing my worries in the creek and watching them float away. For that stretch of my walk, every time a worry creeps into my mind, I toss it in the creek and simply enjoy my walk and the beauty around me. By giving your hyperactive worry muscles a rest, you can focus on truly enjoying the moment.

If you are a worrier, another idea you may find helpful is to designate a specific time to worry. I know this sounds kind of silly. In fact, I chuckle at the image of someone writing "worry" in their schedule book like one more item in their to-do list for the day. Yet this can help you limit the amount of time you spend on this rather unproductive and stress-producing habit. I used this technique recently when I had a misunderstanding with a student. I found myself replaying the situation in my mind over and over again. It was causing me a lot of stress. So I decided I would think about the incident on my way to work and that was it. When the situation crept into my mind again I simply acknowledged it and then dismissed it, saying to myself, "Margie, you already spent your designated worry time today, so let it go." OK, laugh if you will, but if it works for me it can work for you too.

So I am working on worrying less. Posted on my refrigerator is this little poem from *Apples of Gold* (compiled by Jo Petty and published by The C. R. Gibson Company):

Worry never climbed a hill
Worry never paid a bill
Worry never dried a tear
Worry never calmed a fear
Worry never darned a heel
Worry never cooked a meal
Worry never led a horse to water
Worry never done a thing you'd think it oughta.

My prayer for today is this: God, help us to trust in you; to have faith that you will care for us. Let the lilies of the field and the birds in the air serve as reminders of your loving care.

Message to Remember
Worry is a psychological response to stressful situations in your life. Through trusting in God, you can learn to let go of worry. Truly trusting in God gives you peace in knowing that only the Savior holds your tomorrows.

Start Today
Make a list of all the things you worry about. When you have finished, with a smile on your face, tear the paper into little pieces and throw it in the garbage. Or, if you are feeling creative, make a paper airplane out of the list and let your worries fly away. Don't just think about it. Do it.

Evening Reflections

Think about the one thing in your life that you worry the most about and be specific. What has worrying done to help?

What one thing could you do to eliminate or reduce your worry? Are you willing to do this? Think about the message from I Peter 3:10-11: "Those who desire life / and desire to see good days . . . let them seek peace and pursue it."

"Do not worry about anything, but in everything by prayer and supplication with thanksgiving let your requests be made known to God. And the peace of God, which surpasses all understanding, will guard your hearts and your minds in Christ Jesus" (Philippians 4:6-7).

Tonight try letting your cares and concerns be made known to God and leave them in the Creator's hands.

$\mathcal{S}$OURCES OF STRESS

Come to me, all you that are weary and are carrying heavy burdens, and I will give you rest. Take my yoke upon you, and learn from me; for I am gentle and humble in heart, and you will find rest for your souls. For my yoke is easy, and my burden is light. (Matthew 11:28-30)

hile many of us assume that major upheavals such as the death of a spouse or the purchase of a new home cause the greatest stress, a study at the University of California, Berkeley, indicates that everyday aggravations may take the greatest toll. Researchers found that the cumulative stress of such hassles as housework, irritating noise, too many responsibilities, constant interruptions, and rising prices can outweigh that of a major trauma. Seemingly trivial problems that each of us face daily may add up to a serious stress load when each problem is added to the previous one.

There are more sources of stress than we could ever discuss here. Usually, if you stop to think about it, it is fairly easy to identify the things that cause you stress. Knowing what to do about those stressors is another matter. Psychosocial factors, biologic factors, self-imposed factors, and environmental factors can all contribute to your stress response.

Every single day you are confronted with situations that cause you to be stressed. Let's look briefly at a few of these psychosocial factors.

Change—Anytime your routine is disrupted or unexpected change occurs you are likely to experience stress. Your stress level may increase with the increase in the changes and adaptations that you must make. Drs. Thomas Holmes and Richard Rahe determined, based on their research, that certain events predict increased risk for illness. They found that people who reported the most change in their lives—either positive or negative—also seemed to suffer the most illnesses. Their "Social Readjustment Rating Scale" has been used extensively as an indicator of stress overload and potential illness.

Think about the fact that some individuals have faced repeated disasters and drastic changes, and yet because of their personalities and attitudes, they appear to be immune to stress. I am reminded of Viktor Frankl, Viennese psychoanalyst and Holocaust survivor, who emphasized that while individuals may be powerless to modify their environments or even their physical condition, each person does have the ultimate power to fashion their reactions and find interior meaning, even in the most difficult circumstances.

So, while many changes in your life may increase your stress level, not everyone responds to change in the same manner.

Pressure—The Army ad says, "Be all that you can be." It sounds like a good idea, but the constant challenge to be more and better can be overwhelming. You may feel a great deal of pressure to look a certain way, to maintain a certain standard of living, to live up to others' expectations, to get better grades, to earn more money, and on and on. Step back and think about what is important to you. What do *you* want?

The simple fact is that we just plain overload ourselves with too many responsibilities. Have you ever longed to take a weekend or even a day off to stay home and read a good book; to sleep in and stay in your pajamas all day long; to take time to visit with friends and not feel guilty? If you can not remember the last time you took time off for yourself, you are overloaded and burnout will not be far behind. Think about this advice, "Do your best, leave the rest."

Isn't it interesting that we use time out as a punishment for children, yet most adults would love some time each day to sit quietly and think about what they are doing. How very important it is that we take time out each day! When I talk to people about how they cope with stress, many mention taking time to be alone and to engage in solitary activities they find renew their mind and spirit. Matt said, "Each day I find time to go for a walk first thing in the morning. This nourishes my body, mind, and spirit." Barb mentioned taking time to read, especially books of a spiritual nature.

Hassles—While major changes in your life may cause stress, recent research has indicated that those daily minor annoyances may have an even greater impact on your well-being. We all have these hassles—locking your keys in the car, sitting in traffic, finding out at the end of the day that you've had a piece of spinach stuck in your front tooth, misplacing your address book, a boss who never gives a compliment. Hassles are constant everyday stressors that can become chronic and result in long-term effects. It is the cumulative effect of these minor hassles that may be harmful in the long run. The good news is that while hassles are unavoidable in day-to-day living, we can take action to reduce or manage their impact.

Isolation—Feelings of loneliness and isolation can certainly be a source of stress. In our highly mobile society many people find themselves separated from family and friends. Feeling connected and supported by people you care about can help you cope with stress. I would like to share a story with you to demonstrate the importance in my life of feeling connected.

Sitting in our living room is a coffee table that belonged to my Grandma and Grandpa Calloway before they died. My husband recently had the coffee table restored for me and it is one of my most valued pieces of furniture. While the table is not valuable in dollars and cents, it is very valuable to me because of the memories and message it holds. It serves as a reminder to me that I am connected to a loving family. I am very blessed to have grown up in a family where I was surrounded by grandparents, aunts, uncles, cousins, brothers, sisters, and loving parents.

The coffee table, for as long as I can remember, held a prominent spot in Grandma and Grandpa's living room. What made this coffee table so special was that under the glass top Grandma had a collage of pictures of their family—their five children, twenty grandchildren, thirty-six great grandchildren, and four great-great grandchildren. With each new birth and with each marriage, the family increased and new photos were added until every tiny space on that coffee table was covered with a smiling face. Today the pictures on the coffee table have changed but the message has stayed the same: It is important to feel loved and connected.

Look back over the psychosocial factors that contribute to stress. Think about the ones that most affect you. After you examine and recognize the stressors in your life, the next step is to examine the situation carefully and consider your options. You can
1. alter the circumstances to eliminate or reduce the cause of stress, or
2. change your behavior and reaction to the stressful events in your life.

In section three, you will learn specific tools to guide you in changing your responses to stressful situations by either taking mental action to change your thinking or by taking physical action to combat the physical effects of stress.

Message to Remember
Changes, pressures, daily hassles, and isolation are psychosocial factors that can have a major impact on your health. Recognizing these sources of stress will help you identify how to manage them.

Start Today
Complete the "Social Readjustment Rating Scale" at the end of this chapter. This is one of many tools that may help you understand stress in your life.

Evening Reflections

"'For I was hungry and you gave me food, I was thirsty and you gave me something to drink, I was a stranger and you welcomed me, I was naked and you gave me clothing, I was sick and you took care of me, I was in prison and you visited me.' " Then the righteous will answer him, 'Lord, when was it that we saw you hungry and gave you food, or thirsty and gave you something to drink? And when was it that we saw you a stranger and welcomed you, or naked and gave you clothing? And when was it that we saw you sick or in prison and visited you?' And the king will answer them, 'Truly I tell you, just as you did it to one of the least of these who are members of my family, you did it to me'" (Matthew 25:35-40).

This scripture reminds us that we are connected to others. We are all part of God's family.

People who generally handle stress well feel this connection to others, to families, to friends, even to strangers. They sense that they are part of something bigger and that they belong. Can you reach out to someone who feels lonely or isolated? If you feel alone, can you reach out to connect to others?

"And let the peace of Christ rule in your hearts, to which indeed you were called in the one body. And be thankful" (Colossians 3:15). Think about the one body—the church. Be thankful for this blessing.

Begin thinking about goals that you would like to see take shape in your life so that you can live more abundantly and peacefully. In section four you will learn more about planning and taking action for the life you desire.

Social Readjustment Rating Scale

Life Event	Life Change Units
Death of a spouse	100
Divorce	73
Marital separation	65
Jail term	63
Death of a close family member	63
Personal injury or illness	53
Marriage	50
Fired at work	47
Marital reconciliation	45
Retirement	45
Change in health of family member	44
Pregnancy	40
Sexual dysfunction	39
Gain of a new family member	39
Business readjustment	39
Change in financial status	38
Death of a close friend	37
Change to different line of work	36
Change in number of arguments with spouse	35
Mortgage over $10,000	31
Foreclosure of mortgage or loan	30
Change in responsibilities at work	29
Son or daughter leaving home	29
Trouble with in-laws	29
Outstanding personal achievement	28
Spouse begins or stops work	26
Begin or end school	26
Change in living conditions	25
Revision of personal habits	24
Trouble with boss	23
Change in work hours or conditions	20
Change in residence	20
Change in schools	20
Change in recreation	19
Change in church activities	19
Change in social activities	18
Mortgage or loan less than $10,000	17

Change in sleeping habits	16
Change in number of family get-togethers	15
Change in eating habits	13
Vacation	13
Christmas	12
Minor violation of the law	11

Check off those events that currently apply to your life and add up the corresponding points or Life-Change Units. A score below 150 is thought to be within the range of normal stress. A score between 150 and 199 suggests a mild life crisis; between 200 and 299 points suggests a moderate life crisis; above 300 points is indicative of a major life crisis.

Reprinted from Journal of Psychosomatic Research, vol. 11, by T. H. Holmes and R. Rahe, The Social Readjustment Rating Scale, pp. 213-218, 1967, with permission from Elsevier Science.

Section 3 Chapter 15

$\mathcal{D}$EEP BREATHING

Thus says the Lord GOD to these bones: I will cause breath to enter you, and you shall live. (Ezekiel 37:5)

$\mathcal{W}$elcome to section three. As we continue our journey to a more peaceful life, let us take a minute to review our progress. In section one we explored important ideas for getting started, such as the importance of your perception and the process of making changes. The focus of section two was understanding stress—assessing your stress, the physical and emotional consequences of too much stress, and the sources of stress. Now it is time to get down to the business of learning effective techniques for relieving stress. In the next few chapters we will explore physical strategies for calming the body (deep breathing, progressive muscle relaxation, stretching, and exercise) and mental strategies for calming the mind (mental imagery, meditation, and cognitive techniques). Practice these approaches and decide which ones work best for you.

You know now that stress is part of life. It is not going to go away. The question is how can you learn to manage your stress and enjoy a more balanced and abundant life? As Hans Selye suggests, "I cannot and should not be cured of my stress, but merely taught to enjoy it."

When you are deciding which stress relief techniques work best for you, think about the symptoms of too much stress in your body. If you are troubled with muscle tension, then stretching or progressive muscle relaxation might work best. If worry, anxiety, and fear are your most troublesome symptoms, then cognitive techniques, mental imagery or meditation might work best for you. Choose a technique or a combination of techniques to create the very best plan for you.

Deep Breathing

Deep breathing, also known as diaphragmatic breathing, is one of the easiest, most effective, and most accessible methods for relaxation. You can learn to slow yourself down by conscious deep breathing. This is so effective it is incorporated into nearly every other method of relaxation.

Many of us are primarily chest, or thoracic, breathers. This normal breathing involves mostly the chest and thoracic muscles. Diaphragmatic, or abdominal, breathing involves the movement of the abdomen as well. This deep breathing allows us to take in more oxygen with each breath. Normally, you will take in twelve to sixteen breaths each minute. In a relaxed state, with deep breathing, the number of breaths can be comfortably reduced to as few as four. Deep breathing slows your entire nervous system in direct opposition to the stress response that speeds it up.

It is interesting that children start out as abdominal breathers and shift to thoracic breathing as they mature. Some experts think this is learned behavior since when we sleep and are without the influences of our conscious mind we revert to deeper abdominal breathing.

Try this activity to see if you are a chest breather. First, breathe out and empty your lungs. Count to three and inhale deeply. Now, hold it. Did your shoulders go up? Do you feel like the upper part of your lungs are most full? If so, you probably lean towards chest breathing. If you are a diaphragmatic breather, you would feel your abdominal area expand, your belt tighten, and fullness in the lower part of your chest.

Try these steps for deep breathing:

1. Get Comfortable

Find a comfortable quiet place to practice this technique. Try lying on your back with a small pillow under your head and your eyes closed. Loosen your clothing, especially around your neck and abdomen. Fold your hands across your lower chest so your little fingers rest just above your navel. Take a slow, deep breath. Your stomach and hands should rise as you breathe in. Your fingers might slide apart slightly. As you exhale, your hands should sink and your fingers glide together.

2. Concentrate

Normal breathing is for the most part an unconscious act regulated by the medulla oblongata of your brain. To get the most from your deep breathing you will want to clear your mind from distractions and focus on the flow of air through your body. Some find it helpful to think about the process, saying to themselves, "The air flows through my nose, traveling deep into my lungs as my stomach rises. As I exhale, my stomach falls, the air flows from my lungs, up my throat and out my mouth." Repeat with each breath.

3. Think of the Steps

Think of each breath as four steps:
1. Bring air into your lungs through your nose or mouth, feel your abdomen rise.
2. Pause slightly before you exhale.
3. Release the air to flow out by the path it entered, feel your abdomen fall.
4. Pause after exhaling.

Repeat the process several times. Feel the tension ease with each breath out. Concentrate on breathing away the tension and breathing in refreshing oxygen and God's breath of life.

After some practice, try a sitting position. The beauty of this relaxation technique is that once you have mastered it you can do it anywhere, anytime—waiting in line at the grocery store, before getting up to give a speech, while sitting in rush hour traffic—whenever you need it.

Message to Remember

Deep breathing is one of the easiest, most effective, and most accessible methods for relaxation.

Start Today

Find a quiet time to practice deep breathing for ten minutes.

Evening Reflection

Did you practice deep breathing today? How did you feel? Could you feel your worries and cares leaving and the life-giving breath of God entering as you practiced the exercise?

Do you have quiet time to sit and breathe during the day? Every day? If not, how can you incorporate it into your daily life?

Think about being nice to yourself this week. You deserve to be pampered.

Tonight as you prepare for sleep, think about God breathing new life and energy into your body. Think about feeling refreshed, restored, and invigorated. Think about breathing out the tension, fear, worry, and doubt that can build inside you. Take five deep cleansing breaths before you sleep. End your day in prayer, "Breathe on me breath of God, fill me with life anew."

PROGRESSIVE MUSCLE RELAXATION

Be still, and know that I am God! (Psalm 46:10)

The most common symptom of stress is muscle tension. This makes sense because your body responds to stress by exciting your muscles. Your muscles are ready for action to protect you from danger—remember, fight or flight!

With Progressive Muscle Relaxation (PMR) you learn to systematically tense and then relax the muscle groups throughout your body to reduce muscle tension. Research has proven that it works to help your body manage the effects of stress.

Dr. Edmund Jacobson developed this technique to help patients suffering from muscle tension associated with stress. Since nearly all his patients, regardless of illness, experienced muscle tension, Dr. Jacobson believed that if people could reduce muscle tension, their susceptibility to disease would decrease.

His three step technique is simple:
>First, tense a muscle group.
>Second, relax the muscle group.
>Third, concentrate on the feelings associated with tension and relaxation.

Dr. Jacobson proposed that teaching an individual to identify the difference in feeling between the tensed muscle and the relaxed muscle would promote a deepened sense of relaxation.

Like any new skill, PMR takes practice. It is quite simple to learn, however, and many people find this technique very beneficial as part of their stress management regime. A word of caution: the isometric muscle contractions used in PMR can increase your blood pressure. If you have high blood pressure, check with your health care provider before trying this technique.

PMR—The Basic Steps:
1. Start with the muscle groups in your lower extremities and move up to the head or reverse the order and begin with your head and move down, whichever feels best to you.
2. Isolate a muscle group and contract those muscles, leaving all other muscles relaxed.
3. Contract the muscle groups on both sides of the body simultaneously. For example, contract the muscles in both feet at the same time.
4. Hold the contraction for 10-15 seconds, then relax your body for 20-30 seconds before going on to the next muscle group.
5. Focus attention on the intensity of the contraction. Imagine the muscle getting tighter and tighter.
6. During the relaxation phase for each muscle group concentrate on the feeling of relaxation, comparing it to how the muscle felt when it was tensed. Try imagining a warm light flowing through your body as your muscles become soft and relaxed.

Begin by lying on the floor, with your arms at your side, palms facing down. A quiet, dark room promotes relaxation. Inhale as you contract the muscles and exhale as you release the tension. Focus on the feelings of relaxation when the tension is released.

Progress through each muscle group one at a time, tightening and then relaxing—your feet, calves, thighs, buttocks, lower back, abdomen, hands and forearms, chest, shoulders, neck, jaw, and face.

Not sure how to contract these muscle groups? Try this:
Face—Squint your eyes, pull your forehead toward your nose.
Jaws—Clench your jaw.

Neck—Isolate the muscle of your neck from your head and shoulders, tense your neck muscles (lots of muscle tension here).

Shoulders—Tighten your shoulder muscles (lots of muscle tension stored here too).

Upper chest—Isolate your chest muscles; feel the muscles tighten around your ribs.

Hands and forearms —Make a fist as tight as you can.

Abdominals—Tense your stomach muscles.

Lower back—Try to press your lower back to the floor and hold it tightly.

Buttocks—Squeeze the gluteal (rear-end) muscles as tightly as you can.

Thighs—Isolate your thigh muscles from your abdominals and buttocks and tense tightly.

Calves—Point your toes.

Feet— Scrunch your toes tightly.

Once you are good at PMR you can do it almost anywhere. I like to do it in bed to relax before I fall asleep. You can do it at your desk, on the way to work (a little tricky if you are driving), or at home to help unwind for the evening. Feel free to adapt the technique. For example, some prefer to start at the head and work down or you might want to try it sitting. Whatever works for you.

Today there are several versions of this technique and many show similar positive results. Most people feel some benefits after each session with accumulating physiological benefits after a few weeks. Jacobson recommends three 5-minute sessions daily to achieve the full benefits of PMR. How about substituting a PMR break for one of your coffee breaks?

Message to Remember

Muscle tension is a very common response to stress. Progressive muscle relaxation is a wonderful way to relax muscle groups throughout your body.

Start Today

Try combining your deep breathing techniques from yesterday with PMR. Begin by lying on the floor. Do a full body stretch—stretch your arms above you and make your body as long as you can. Next, do deep breathing for two or three minutes followed by progressive muscle relaxation.

Evening Reflection

Think about the feeling of relaxation from PMR. This relaxation technique gets better with practice, so the more you do it the better the results. Is this a technique you would like to continue?

This evening try this activity from *Pack Up Your Gloomees in a Great Big Box* by Barbara Johnson. First read the line and then consciously experience the outcome.

Be Still and Know That I Am God

Be still, **my muscles,** and know God's *relaxation.*
Be still, **my nerves,** and know God's *rest.*
Be still, **my heart,** and know God's *quietness.*
Be still, **my body,** and know God's *renewal.*
Be still, **my mind,** and know God's *peace.*

"Be still, and know that I am God!" (Psalm 46:10).

Section 3 Chapter 17

$\mathscr{S}$TRETCHING

Beloved, I pray that all may go well with you and that you may be in good health, just as it is well with your soul. (3 John 2)

$\mathscr{H}$ave you ever watched a cat stretch? Our cat, Pepe, takes frequent stretch breaks. Now in Pepe's case I truly doubt that he is stretching to relax tense muscles. The most stressful part of his daily routine is deciding what goofy new place to take a nap after one of his numerous snack breaks. We human types have a few more demands on us than Pepe's eat, sleep, and stretch existence. As you have already learned, one of your automatic physical responses to stress is muscle tension. Stretching is a simple, easy way to relax tense muscles.

First, let us look at the proper way to stretch and a couple of cautions before you begin.

- Never jerk or force a stretch. Stretching should never be painful.
- Slowly stretch until you feel a pleasant lengthening of the muscle. Then, while exhaling, stretch just a little farther.
- Hold the stretch for about 30 seconds and relax.
- For greatest benefit repeat the exercise two or three times.

I have included a few stretches in this chapter that are especially helpful for stress-related muscle tension. My intent is not to provide a total muscle-stretching program. You may want to refer to a stretching book for more ideas. As with any exercise program that is new to you, check with your health professional before starting these exercises.

Morning Stretch

When you first wake up in the morning try easing into the day with some gentle stretches. After a night's sleep, your heart rate is slow, your body temperature is relatively low, your muscles and joints may be stiff, and your mind is not yet fully alert. Rather than jump out of bed and head straight for the coffeepot, take five minutes to perform a series of morning stretches. These stretches can help ease you into the day and help you maintain a sense of relaxation throughout the day. You might want to combine your stretches with your morning prayers.

- Lie on your back and extend your hands toward the ceiling. Reach toward the ceiling and hold that stretch. Then slowly lower your hands in an arc above your head until they lie flat on the mattress. Point your toes and elongate your body for a full-body stretch.
- Lift your right leg and point your toes toward the ceiling until your feel the stretch in the back of your leg. Hold. Repeat the stretch with your left leg.
- Remain on your back and grasp your right knee. Draw it gently toward your chest. Hold. Repeat the stretch with your left leg.
- Pull both knees to your chest. Hold.
- Sit on the side of the bed. Shrug your shoulders toward your ears. Hold. Then relax and let your shoulders fall.

Stretch Break

The stretches on pages 77 and 78 require only a few minutes at work or at home during coffee or lunch breaks.

Back Stretch
Stretch forward, rest your body on your lap, and relax your head and neck. Hold for about a minute, then press on your thighs to sit back up.

Leg Stretch
With one foot on a support, slowly lean forward. Bend from your hips, and keep your back straight. Repeat 5 times on each leg.

Neck Stretch
Without moving your shoulders, slowly rotate your head forward, then back to center; left, then back to center; right, then back to center. Hold each for 30 seconds.

Shoulder and Arm Stretch
With fingers interlaced, stretch overhead with palms upward. Hold 30 seconds, relax, and repeat 5 times.

Upper Body Stretch
With your feet comfortably apart, reach overhead and stretch to the side. (Try not to move your hips.) Hold for 30 seconds, then switch sides.

Passive Back Stretch
Lie on the floor with your legs on a chair. Press your lower back onto the floor. Rest in this position for several minutes.

Message to Remember

Muscle tension is one of your automatic physical responses to stress. Stretching is a quick and easy way to reduce muscle tension.

Start Today

Practice the morning stretches and the stretch break exercises. You may want to add some additional stretches that feel good to you.

Evening Reflection

How did it feel to stretch your muscles? Remember, stretching should not be painful. Think of each muscle as being like a rubber band. Stretching the muscle encourages blood flow and helps keep the muscle pliable and healthy.

Reflect back on today's scripture reading: "Beloved, I pray that all may go well with you and that you may be in good health, just as it is well with your soul" (3 John 2).

Brainstorm on ways you can glorify God in your physical body by taking steps to be healthier.

Proverbs 10:17 tells us: "Whoever heeds instruction is on the path to life. . ." Prayerfully consider God's will for your physical body. If God wrote an instruction manual on caring for your body, what advice do you think it would contain? Ask for God's help as you care for your body.

*E*XERCISE: MOVE YOUR BODY

Since we have these promises, beloved, let us cleanse ourselves from every defilement of body and of spirit, making holiness perfect in the fear of God. (2 Corinthians 7:1)

*P*hysical movement, exercise, is one of the most effective and natural ways to reduce stress. It makes sense when you understand that the stress response gears up the body for action. In response to stress, your body is flooded with hormones that prepare you for action. Your heart rate increases, blood pressure rises, breathing speeds up, and blood is redistributed to the working muscles. To release the effects of stress, you need to move your body. Think back to how our ancestors used the energy of the stress response to either fight or flee. Exercise produces the same results for you.

When you do not provide a physical release for the effects of stress, your body begins to wear down. It is like driving your car with the brakes on. Your body is working against itself. The body's natural inclination in response to stress is to be active, to move. Remaining inactive puts a great strain on your internal systems.

There are many physical activities that can help you cope with stress. Some excellent stress-relieving activities are walking, jogging, bicycling, and swimming. These are all examples of aerobic exercises. Aerobic exercises may be the most powerful anti-stress therapy you can practice. Aerobic exercises help your body use oxygen more efficiently, and they are an excellent way to bring your stress hormones back into balance. Even the simple act of brisk walking discharges energy and begins to calm mind and body.

The interesting paradox is that you get energy by expending energy. Aerobic exercise makes your body more oxygen efficient, so you consume less oxygen even when you go about your normal activities. Exercise also increases your metabolic rate, which in turn increases your body's overall efficiency. According to cardiologist Dr. James Rippe, "It's like improving the size of your engine. If your engine is capable of doing 150 miles an hour, then when you're going 25 miles an hour, you're using less capacity." Rippe goes on to say, "One of the chief reasons exercise is such an energizer is that it makes us feel calm and at peace."

Engaging in twenty to thirty minutes of aerobic exercise three to four times a week will help reduce the effects of stress. Recent research suggests that exercising in five-minute blocks of time followed by relaxation techniques can be even more beneficial for relieving stress than a thirty-minute workout.

Here is Mary's stress story:

My mother became a mother and a wife at seventeen. Three more children came along later. She did an excellent job raising her kids, keeping her home clean, and being a devoted wife. But when stress arose, she just didn't know how to handle it.

Mom would go down to the bar with a few friends, and at first it wasn't a problem. It soon became a habit for Mom to cope with her stressors by drowning them in alcohol. Some nights she would drink until the sun came up, but no matter how rough the night had been, Mom would always see us off to school in the morning.

Finally, one day Mom realized that the alcohol was causing more stress than it was relieving. She joined an AA group and started running for exercise. There were many times she would become really stressed and want to drink, but she was rigid about fighting off her addiction.

If she comes under a stressful situation now, she knows to call a good friend and talk or to go for a quick run. In a way, running has replaced her drinking. Last year Mom ran a marathon. But more importantly, she has been sober for five years. I'm sure proud of my mom.

Not only are there physical benefits of exercise, but psychological benefits as well. Studies indicate that people who participate in regular exercise report higher levels of self-esteem and lower incidences of anxiety and depression. Once again we are reminded that the body, mind, and spirit work together as one entity.

Exercise also may reduce stress by increasing the level of endorphins in the bloodstream. Endorphins are mood-lifting chemicals that produce a natural high. As a result, exercise can increase your energy, reduce hostility, improve mental alertness, and help you cope more effectively with stress. A physician friend once told me that if all the benefits of exercise could be put in a pill form, it would be the most prescribed pill in this country. The benefits of exercise are many.

Sarah, a twenty-one-year old student, started taking brisk daily walks to help herself stop smoking. She kicked the habit—and more. An unexpected benefit of her regular walking program is that Sarah has better control of her moods and emotions. She reports, "Walking helped me with my anxiety and I feel more confident in dealing with my problems."

So if exercise is so great, why don't we do it? A recent survey of men and women aged forty and older found that, although almost all believed in the importance of exercise, 41 percent of the women and 33 percent of the men did not exercise at all. The problem may be due to our attitude about exercise.

Do you think of exercise as a punishment or a privilege? as something you have to do or something you get to do? For stress management, you can get amazing results from simply incorporating a total of twenty to thirty minutes of moderate activity into your daily routine. This can include activities such as brisk walking, gardening, or climbing stairs. This is a race won by the tortoise, not the hare. Pushing yourself to go harder, faster, farther is not the answer to stress-relieving exercise.

Learning to use physical activity to complement mental and emotional strategies can alleviate stress most effectively.

Message to Remember

Physical activity allows your body to use stress hormones constructively for their intended purpose. Aerobic exercise has positive physical and psychological benefits.

Start Today

Try some aerobic exercise today. What you decide to do will depend on your interests and previous exercise history. If you are able, take a brisk fifteen-minute walk outdoors. Consider giving yourself the gift of regular exercise.

Evening Reflection

Think about your attitude and beliefs about exercise. Is it something you want to do or something you have to do? How important is physical activity to you? Do you make it a priority on a regular basis?

Moving in Joy

"...The joy of the LORD is your strength" (Nehemiah 8:10).

How easily the child played
Running, skipping, jumping, giggling
A child's job, employing body, mind and spirit
Experiencing joy.

The child matured, and jobs turned to drudgery
No time to play.
Weary mind and soul fed on potato chips and pizza
And TV.

"You should exercise!" he heard society say.
That word, too, connoted drudgery and work
Funny clothes and sweating a lot
So he didn't.

But the everlasting child in him longed to play
Longed to move for the joy of it.
One day a friend said, "Walk with me!"
So he did.

They kicked leaves and watched the sun set and laughed.
Muscle and sinew remembered that moving felt good.
Nature, laughter and friendship fed mind and spirit.
It didn't seem like exercise.

The friends set a daily time
Not to exercise
But to walk and laugh
and experience joy. *

Be thankful for the joy of movement. Thanks to my friend Ronnette Sailors for sharing *Moving in Joy* with me.

Plan ways that you could incorporate physical activity in your life so that it is fun and enjoyable. One lesson I have learned in my work in health promotion is that we humans seek out those things that bring us pleasure. Make exercise a pleasurable experience. The people who stay with exercise are those who make it a positive activity. While it definitely was not the case when I first started a regular exercise program nearly twenty years ago, I have come to think of exercise as a gift I give myself each day. I look forward to it.

Reflect on the connection between discipline with your physical body and discipline in your spiritual life. Do you think there is a connection? Could discipline in one area enhance discipline in the other?

---

* Used by permission, Health Ministries, Alegent Health, 7500 Mercy Road, Omaha NE 68124

*M*ENTAL IMAGERY

Those of steadfast mind you keep in peace— / in peace because they trust in you. (Isaiah 26:3)

*Y*our brain is truly a miraculous organ. Your thinking and imagination have a profound impact on the quality of your life. Imagination is like a two-edged sword when it comes to stress. On one hand, your imagination can go wild creating *what if* situations. Many of these imagined situations never develop, but the resulting stress response can be very real. On the other hand, you can use your imagination to create a calm, peaceful place in your mind. This relaxation response created by your imagination is equally real.

We have explored physical strategies for calming the body. Now we will look at mental strategies for calming the mind. A quiet mind does not happen automatically.

Close your eyes and imagine your favorite peaceful scene, perhaps a mountain stream, a star-filled night, a tropical island, or a path through a dense pine forest. Images of water—ocean waves, waterfalls, mountain streams—often promote relaxation. The image will be different for each person. One man told me he imagined sitting in Central Park on a cool, sunny day with the smell of hot dogs and the sounds of children playing.

Your belief that the scene you visualize will promote tranquility creates the relaxation response. Enhance the experience by involving all your senses. Not only visualize the scene, but also hear the sounds, feel the air, the wind, the sun on your skin, and smell the fragrances. Become an active participant in your image.

Below is an imagery script adapted from *The Spirit of Synergy* by Robert Keck. I find this especially relaxing and soothing. You may want to create your own imagery script or purchase a relaxation tape.

- *Sit upright and well back in your chair so that your thighs and back are supported, and rest your hands in the cradled position on your lap, or, if you prefer, lightly on top of your thighs. Let your feet rest on the ground just beneath your knees.*
- *Close your eyes gently. Settle down comfortably. Begin by breathing out first. Then breathe in easily just as much as you need to. Now breathe out slowly with a slight sigh like a balloon slowly deflating. Do this once more, very slowly, and as you breathe out feel the tension begin to drain away. Then go back to your ordinary breathing—even, quiet, and steady.*
- *Allow yourself to relax very deeply, letting go of tension or concerns in body, mind, and spirit and trusting in the presence of God in the very depths of your being.*
- *Now direct your thoughts to each part of your body, to your muscles and joints.*
- *Think first about your left foot. Your toes are relaxed and still. Your foot is resting easily on the floor.*
- *Now focus on your right foot, right toes, right ankle.*
- *Think now about your legs. Become aware of the muscles in your thighs, letting those bigger muscles of the legs relax until they become very loose and limp.*
- *Your back muscles will relax when you hold yourself easily upright and let the back of the chair support the spine.*
- *Let your abdominal muscles become soft and relaxed. There is no need to hold your stomach in tightly. It rises and falls as you breathe quietly.*
- *Think about your fingers of your left hand. They are curved, limp, and still. Now focus on the fingers of your right hand; relaxed, soft, and still. This feeling of relaxation spreads up your arms to your shoulders.*
- *Let your shoulders relax. Let them drop easily. Now let them relax even farther than you thought they could.*

- *Your neck muscles will relax if your head is held upright, resting easily balanced on the top of your spine, or supported against the back of the chair.*
- *Let your face relax. Let the expression leave it.*
- *Make sure your teeth are not held tightly together and let your jaw rest in its relaxed position.*
- *Your cheeks are soft because there is no need to keep up an expression. Your lips are soft and hardly touching.*
- *Relax your forehead so that it feels a little wider and a little higher than before.*
- *Now, instead of thinking of yourself in parts, become aware of the all-over sensation of letting go, of quiet, and rest.*
- *When your muscles are relaxed, you begin to feel peaceful, rested, and quiet.*
- *Imagine yourself outside on a lazy summer day, walking beside a river. You stop to notice wildflowers on the way or the water flowing over rocks at the bank. Be aware of the plants, dirt, rocks, breeze. Feel connected to the sounds and smells and sights of nature all around you.*
- *As you stroll along, you reach a soft grassy area along the bank. Lie down and allow yourself to feel lazy and calm. Feeling a deep sense of harmony with everything around you, you even doze off now and then. Time passes. You become aware that darkness has fallen and that a vast, black sky sprinkled with twinkling stars is above you. You give thanks for the incredible beauty of this vast universe, and you are grateful at the very core of your being.*
- *You are aware that you are in the presence of the God that created the universe and that you are a part of all you see and sense. But you are also special, unique, created by God to be you. Recognize the wonder you are feeling.*
- *Let your eyes rest on one star and follow its light all the way to earth. Feel that light literally touch your body, enter it, flow through every blood vessel into each cell of your body. Let yourself rejoice in knowing that you are unique and you are a part of the vast universe. Let yourself experience the security of knowing that you are at home with the God that has created everything, that you are loved and accepted exactly as you are. God's love is given to you; you have nothing to earn. Just be, knowing that you are loved. Bask in this presence with God.*
- *After a while, knowing that you can return to this spot whenever you*

like, begin to leave it. Go slowly, taking with you this sense of being at home with God, this sense of being a part of the vast universe that God created. Gradually become aware of your external, physical reality even as you keep with you the sense of being accepted and appreciated just as you are.

- *Gradually, and at your own pace, allow your consciousness to rise to the surface. When you are ready to be alert again to your present reality, take a deep breath, blink, and stretch. You should be refreshed and alert.*

With practice, even five minutes of deep relaxation is effective in calming your body and mind.

Message to Remember

Combining muscle relaxation with imagery is a powerful strategy for deep relaxation.

Start Today

Find a quiet place and time to practice mental imagery. Ask someone to read the script to you while you do it, or record it on an audio cassette so that you can play it back anytime. Try reading through the imagery a few times, and then practice with your own adaptations.

Take a walk again today. Why not make this a habit?

Evening Reflection

Let me ask you a question: What do you think God envisions for you each day? Do you think it is unrest, stress, strife, anger, frustration, fear, or doubt? God's word tells us in Jeremiah 29:11-12: "For surely I know the plans I have for you, says the LORD, plans for your welfare and not for harm, to give you a future with hope. Then when you call upon me and come and pray to me, I will hear you."

Write your own mental imagery script. Tonight, as you drift off to sleep, begin to imagine your peaceful scene.

*M*EDITATION

Let the words of my mouth and the meditation of my heart / be acceptable to you, / O LORD, my rock and my redeemer. (Psalm 19:14)

*M*editation is a way of quieting your mind, of clearing the mental chatter. We are continuously bombarded with mental stimulation. Meditation allows us to temporarily tune out, to relieve ourselves of both internal and external stress. Think of meditation as a strategy to gain control over your thoughts.

There are many forms of meditation and there is no single right way to meditate. Experiment to find the approach that works best for you. Most forms of meditation involve these common elements: sitting quietly for twenty to thirty minutes, deep breathing, repetition of a word or phrase or focus on an object, and concentrating on self-awareness. The important element is narrowing your focus.

Cardiologist Dr. Herbert Benson, in his book *The Relaxation Response*, suggests four steps to promote relaxation through meditation.

1. **A quiet environment.** An important element of meditation is reduced sensory stimulation. If it is difficult for you to find a totally quiet environment try using white noise such as soft instrumental music.
2. **A mental device.** A mental device provides a focal point on which to direct all your attention. Its purpose is to replace all

other thoughts. A mantra (a word or phrase you repeat) may be helpful. Commonly used mantras include the syllable "om" and the words *one, peace,* and *calm.* You may find that combining a mantra with diaphragmatic breathing is effective. Repeat your mantra as you exhale and draw out the word so it lasts for the entire breath. The word *calm* sounds like ca-a-a-l-l-l-m-m-m.

3. **A passive attitude.** You might think of this as the thinker taking time out to be the observer. Become passively aware without judging or analyzing. It takes practice to clear your mind. As a thought enters your mind just acknowledge it, and let it go.

4. **A comfortable position.** To relax your mind you must relax your body. When you think of meditation, you may imagine a bearded monk sitting high on a mountain with his legs crossed in the lotus position. The lotus position, in which the legs are crossed and folded with each foot resting on the alternate thigh, is the most recognized position. For me (and probably for most of you) a more comfortable position is the half-lotus, with your legs crossed in a comfortable manner. Place your hands on your thighs with palms up, thumb and index finger touching.

Think of meditation as a process to help you live in the present moment for a more tranquil and peaceful state of mind.

Here are some helpful suggestions:
—Early morning is a great time to meditate. Designate time in your schedule.
—Do not meditate on a full stomach and do not meditate lying down.
—Meditate twenty to thirty minutes a day.
—Start your meditation time by repeating the vowels (a, e, i, o, u) in a low, deep, drawn out tone. This helps you begin to narrow your attention and make the transition to a meditative state. Put your hand on your chest and feel the vibration as you say aaaaa, eeeee, iiiii, ooooo, uuuuu. You will feel the change in vibration with each vowel. Focus on the low sound and the feeling of vibration.

Repetitive Prayer

Dr. Benson continued his reseach on stress. He wondered if prayer—especially, repetitive prayer—would bring about the same relaxation response as meditation. Some people had difficulty staying with meditation, and he wanted to explore the idea that they might be more likely to stay with their relaxation routine if they meditated on prayer. He found that repetitive prayer—such as "Hail Mary, full of grace" for Catholics, "Shalom" for Jews, and "Our Father who art in heaven" did bring on the relaxation response. Benson called this finding the faith factor.

Aerobic prayer is a form of repetitive prayer in which you repeat your prayer in cadence with the movement of walking, bicycling, or running. What a great way to involve your body, mind, and spirit in relaxation!

Breath Prayer

A form of meditation that I have found particularly comforting is the Breath Prayer. In his book, *The Breath of Life*, Ron DelBene describes the breath prayer as a way to be constant in prayer and to feel oneness with God. To discover your breath prayer follow these five easy steps:

Step One

Sit in a comfortable position. Close your eyes, and remind yourself that God loves you and that you are in God's loving presence. Recall a passage from scripture that puts you in a prayerful frame of mind. Consider "The LORD is my shepherd" (Psalm 23:1) or "Be still, and know that I am God!" (Psalm 46:10).

Step Two

With your eyes closed, imagine that God is calling you by name. Hear God asking: "(Your name), what do you want?"

Step Three

Answer God with whatever comes directly from your heart. Your answer might be a single word, such as peace or love or forgiveness. Your answer could be a phrase or brief sentence, such as "I want to feel your forgiveness," or "I want to know your love." Whatever your response is becomes the heart of your prayer.

Step Four

Choose your favorite name for God. Choices commonly made include God, Jesus, Creator, Teacher, Light, Lord, Spirit, Savior, or Shepherd.

Step Five

Combine your name for God with your answer to God's question, "What do you want?" You then have your prayer. For example:

What I want	Name I Call God	Possible Prayer
peace	Lord	Let me know your peace, O Lord.
love	Jesus	Jesus, let me feel your love.
rest	Shepherd	My Shepherd, let me rest in thee.
guidance	Eternal Light	Eternal Light, guide me in your way.

If you have several ideas, eliminate or combine them until you have focused your prayer. You may want many things, but if you think carefully you can narrow your wants to a specific need that you feel is basic to your well-being. Ask yourself, "What do I want that will make me feel most whole?"

When you have gotten to the heart of your needs, search for words that give it expression. Then work with the words until you have a prayer of six to eight syllables. The words should flow smoothly whether spoken aloud or expressed silently as heart thoughts. This is a way to begin to pray unceasingly and feel the nearness of God.

The Breath Prayer is a way to meditate by focusing your thoughts on prayer.

Message to Remember

Meditation is a way to quiet your mind.

Start Today

Create your own Breath Prayer. Identify the specific need that you feel is basic to your well-being. Write it down. Choose your favorite name for God. Write it down. Write your Breath Prayer.

Practice sitting quietly for five minutes repeating your Breath Prayer. Focus on the words and release all other thoughts from your mind.

How about making your walk an "aerobic prayer"?

Evening Reflection

"Cast all your anxiety on him, because he cares for you" (*I Peter 5:7*). As you meditate, choose to let go of your stressful thoughts and your anxiety. Let God fill you with strength, peace, and joy.

"I will call to mind the deeds of the LORD; / I will remember your wonders of old. / I will meditate on all your work, / and muse on your mighty deeds" (Psalm 77: 11-12). Think deeply and with thanksgiving on all God has done for you.

Conclude this day with your Breath Prayer.

$\mathcal{C}$OGNITIVE TECHNIQUES

Search me, O God, and know my heart; / test me and know my thoughts. (Psalm 139:23)

$\mathcal{T}$he last two chapters described mental imagery and meditation as two methods for calming your mind. In this chapter we will look at several ways to use the way you think to relieve stress. We call these cognitive (thinking) techniques. Could simply changing the way you think really reduce your stress? It seems so easy. The way you think—your ideas, values, perceptions—all can affect your stress level.

Cognitive techniques help you change stress-producing thought patterns into thought patterns that will help you cope with stress. You can use these skills to change the way you view difficult situations. So yes, it is simple, but it may not be easy to change the way you think. You might be in the habit of thinking negatively. One study observed parent-child interactions over several days. The researchers found that, on average, there were four hundred negative comments for every positive one spoken to the child. The conclusion was that negative thoughts are actually a learned response that is carried into adulthood.

Think about how you think! Many people who react strongly to mental stress find they have developed self-destructive patterns of thinking. Therapists call this cognitive distortion. Thinking this way can turn meaningless episodes into plagues of anxiety. See if any of these cognitive distortions apply to you.

All-or-Nothing Thinking—You either did the project for work perfectly or you totally messed up. Everything is seen as an extreme (good or bad), and there is no middle ground. "I can't believe I yelled at my kids. I must be a terrible parent."

Personalizing—This is the tendency to assume responsibility for things that are out of your control. "Frank walked right by my desk this morning without saying hello. I must have made him mad." Personalizing can lead to feelings of needless guilt. You constantly ask yourself, *What did I do wrong?* The answer might be *nothing.*

Discounting the Positive—Are you the type who cannot accept a compliment? 'She wouldn't be saying she liked my new dress if I hadn't gained ten pounds."

Assuming the Worst—You know what others are thinking and how things will turn out—and none of it is good. This is also called pessimism. You are sure it will rain on your trip to California. "I think that guy on the bus is staring at me. I must be sprouting a new pimple." He might be thinking you have a great smile.

Making a conscious effort to change or reframe the way you think to focus on more positive ways of thinking is an important element of stress management. The goal is to create positive feelings of challenge rather than negative feelings of threat. Let's look at a few of these techniques.

Thought Stopping

Thought stopping is just what it sounds like. When a negative statement creeps into your mind, you say, *STOP.* Then replace the stress producing negative statement with a positive statement. The key to success is to believe the positive new statement. This may take some practice, but you can actually change the way you think. Suppose you think, "I will never be able to learn how to use this stupid computer; I'm just too old." Say *STOP* and replace the stress-producing thought with, "I am one of the most experienced and mature people in this office. I can do this."

Dr. Larry Tentinger, a colleague, added this idea, "I use *thought starting*. I begin my day—even before I get out of bed—by saying, 'Lord, I do not know what this day holds, but I know you hold the day.' This helps my perspective and serves as a basis from which to relax and trust. This is a great stress reliever for me."

Monitor Self-Talk

Become more aware of the way you talk to yourself. Are you continually putting yourself down? "I'm too fat. No decent woman would ever take a second look at me." "I'm late again. I'll never be able to keep a good job when I can't even get to work on time." "If I weren't such an awful parent, Susie would not have turned to alcohol." This negative thinking, or as it has been called "stinkin thinkin," is largely habit. Try talking to yourself like you would to a friend you love. "You are a smart and capable person. Tomorrow you will schedule to get to work on time." You can see how this positive thinking can help reduce the chronic, nagging stress that eats away at you. Remember, your thoughts generate your feelings. When you think negative thoughts about yourself, your self-esteem is affected and the result is negative emotions such as guilt, anger, anxiety, and fear. Try practicing positive self-talk along with thought stopping. It works!

Power Language

You can boost your feeling of control simply by changing the words you use. Words can create a feeling of powerlessness or a feeling of control. Compare these two statements:

"I can't handle this deadline."

"I won't handle this deadline."

"I won't" is a choice you make—an act of will—resulting in a sense of control rather than helplessness. You are no longer the helpless victim of the events around you.

Be aware today of how often you use the *should* word. "I should stop by and visit Mrs. Jones." "I should probably go for a walk today." "I should start planning for Christmas." "Should" should be eliminated from our vocabulary! Even positive activities take on a burden-like dimension when we use "should." How much better and more in control would you feel if you replaced "should" with "could"? After all, the choice is yours. "I could (or even better, "I choose to") go for a walk today. That would feel so good, and I know I'll be glad I did it."

Don't Sweat the Small Stuff

I saw a T-shirt that said on the front "Don't Sweat the Small Stuff" and on the back "It's All Small Stuff." There is even a book with that title. Of course, this is an over-simplification. We all have to deal with important decisions and choices every day. Some stuff is worth sweating over. The key is in your ability to weed out the trivia. A major source of stress is trying to do too much and trying to store too much data. Decide to forget and let go of unimportant details. As Richard Carlson, author of *Don't Sweat the Small Stuff* says, "When you die, your in-box will not be empty." The message here is that there will always be more to do, so relax, take care of the really important stuff, and let the rest go.

Go With the Flow

There are some things in life that you just cannot change. Learn to bend a little, to be flexible. Remember that the tree that bends in the storm does not break. Think of life as being fluid. There will be difficult and sad times along with the happy times. I think of life as a journey with many hills and valleys along the way. When I am experiencing a difficult and painful time I think of being in the valley. I know I must travel through the valley to reach my destination. I won't be in the valley forever. Then there is the steep and sometimes long climb out of the valley. These parts of the journey test my endurance and strengthen my body and soul. And then, thankfully, there are the mountaintop times. Because I have been in the valley and climbed the hill, I am stronger. I have learned some lessons. I can truly appreciate and enjoy the good times.

I like what psychologist Robert Eliot says, "If you can't fight it or flee it . . . flow with it." Remember his words. Change what you can; flow with what you cannot change.

Think about accepting the things you cannot change. View

challenges as opportunities to grow. Create happiness every day of your life.

Viktor Frankl, psychoanalyst and Holocaust survivor, said, "Everything can be taken from man but one thing—the last human freedom, to choose one's attitude in any given set of circumstances." You may not be able to modify your environment or even your physical condition, but you do have the power to fashion your reactions and to find meaning in even the most difficult circumstances.

Acceptance

A stress management technique that we sometimes overlook is acceptance of situations we can not control. Maybe we tend to overlook it because it is pretty darn difficult to do. Reinhold Niebuhr's *Serenity Prayer* for Alcoholics Anonymous says it eloquently,

"Lord, grant me the serenity to accept the things I cannot change,
the courage to change the things I can,
and the wisdom to know the difference."

So can you actually change the programming in your mind to break the habit of negative, stress-producing thinking? Yes, you can! A great deal of research supports the effectiveness of cognitive techniques on health-related problems associated with stress. The results indicate that in many cases thought processes can be changed to produce better health.

Message to Remember

Through awareness, determination, and practice you can change negative thoughts and feelings of threat into positive feelings of challenge and control.

Start Today

Choose one or two of the cognitive techniques you learned about today and consciously and deliberately use them.

Evening Reflection

Which cognitive techniques did you practice today? You might find it helpful to share with family or friends the cognitive techniques that you are working on. I had shared with our son David that I was working on thought stopping. Later that day we were in the kitchen visiting when he yelled, "Stop!" I quickly realized, after my heart rate returned to normal, that I was presenting a pretty negative view of the topic of conversation. With David's help I was able to rethink my position from a more positive perspective.

In the seven chapters in section three, you have read about several stress relieving techniques. Review these techniques and decide which ones seem best for you. Think about how you can incorporate these into your life.

Oliver Wendell Holmes once said, "Man's mind stretched to a new idea never goes back to its original dimension." Think about the ideas that go into your mind. Consider filling your mind with positive and life-enhancing thoughts. Consider filling your mind with God's holy word.

In prayer tonight, ask God to show you the power of your words and thoughts. Ask God to help you develop a plan to commit the Holy Word to memory and for guidance in removing negative thinking from your mind.

Section 4 Chapter 22

$\mathscr{B}$ALANCED CONTROL

But those who wait for the LORD shall renew their strength, / they shall mount up with wings like eagles, / they shall run and not be weary, / they shall walk and not faint. (Isaiah 40:31)

$\mathscr{I}$n the last seven chapters, we will explore the seven keys to stress less living. What is it about certain people that seems to make them immune to the effects of stress? You all know people who have been faced with overwhelming challenges and stressors in life and yet somehow managed to come through it all with a sense of peace and gratitude. What are the inner resources that allow these individuals to survive and thrive? By increasing your awareness of these keys, you too can become one of these stress less people.

The first key we will explore is control. Studies have shown that feeling a sense of control in life is important to stress management. Control is a very interesting subject. On one hand, we need to be involved, to take control of the things in our life that cause us stress. On the other hand, just about the time we think we have some control and balance in our life, along comes a punch that can knock us right off our feet. Times like this remind us that even if we do everything we know to do, sad and bad things happen that we cannot control. Some things are in our control and some things are not. Balanced living is knowing and acting on what we can change and knowing and letting go of what we cannot change. This reminds me of the saying, "Let go and let God."

Trying to be in control of everything can be a huge stressor. I belong to the Health Ministries Association. This wonderful organization advocates for health and healing in congregations. On the back of their business cards is printed:

> Do not feel totally, personally,
> irrevocably responsible for everything.
> That's my job.
> Love, God

I cannot help thinking about the old Moroccan proverb that goes, "Trust in God, but tie your camel tight." We have a responsibility to be involved and to take control of our lives as best we can, to do our part.

Research indicates that the level of stress we experience is related to the magnitude of control that we are able to exert. So some of the most stressful times in our life are when we feel out of control.

I recently attended a seminar on chronic stress and disease. The speaker said the two most important factors that influence the stress response are predictability and control. The amount of success we have in predicting a stressor (in other words, our ability to see it coming) and the magnitude of control that we are able to exert over the stressor are the most important factors affecting our stress response.

The United Methodist bishop in the Dakotas, Mike Coyner, sends out a regular message over the Internet. Here is an excerpt from *Life in the Dakotas: Forgiveness and Accountability*:

"John Wesley referred to the concept of 'responsible grace'—meaning that God's grace abounds but that we are still responsible for our actions. This term also means that God's grace makes us *response able*, able to respond to God's grace and to live our lives as God intends."

Bishop Coyner's words help clarify the importance of taking responsibility for the things in life that you can control. Focus on being accountable for moving your life in alignment with God's way.

I am reminded of this story from Charles Swindoll's book,

Laugh Again:

There's a preacher who saved up enough money to buy a few inexpensive acres of land. A little run-down, weather-beaten farmhouse sat on the acreage, a sad picture of years of neglect. The land had not been kept up either, so there were old tree stumps, rusted pieces of machinery, and all sorts of debris strewn here and there, not to mention a fence greatly in need of repair. The whole scene was a mess.

During his spare time and his vacations, the preacher rolled up his sleeves and got to work. He hauled off the junk, repaired the fence, pulled away the stumps, and replanted new trees. Then he refurbished the old house into a quaint cottage with a new roof, new windows, new paint job, and finally a few colorful flower boxes. It took several years to accomplish all this, but finally, when the last job had been completed and he was washing up after applying a fresh coat of paint to the mailbox, his neighbor (who had watched all this from a distance) walked over and said, "Well, preacher—looks like you and the Lord have done a pretty fine job on your place here."

Wiping the sweat from his face, the minister replied, "Yeah, I suppose so . . . but you should have seen it when the Lord had it all to Himself."

As Swindoll eloquently goes on to say, "Couldn't God do it all? Of course, He is God—all powerful and all-knowing and all-sufficient. That makes it all the more significant that God prefers to use us in His work. His favorite plan is a combined effort: God plus people equals accomplishment."

That is what I call balanced control. Taking responsibility to do all you can to enhance your well-being combined with the knowledge that some things in life just plain are not in your control. Trust that God will take care of the rest. The principle for living, "Pray as if everything depended on God and work as if everything depended on you," pretty well sums it up.

Turning your life over to God does not mean quitting. Your personal growth starts with a decision to change and a willingness to accept God's help. Balanced control is one of the keys for stress less living.

Message to Remember

Stress less people take control of, and responsibility for, the things they can control. God plus people equals accomplishment.

Start Today

When my husband Jim is faced with a difficult decision he takes out a sheet of paper and writes down the advantages and the disadvantages of each course of action. The best choice is usually much more apparent after this simple activity. Sometimes it helps to write things down.

On a sheet of paper, write in one column the things that are really good about your life. These are the things that make you happy and over which you do not experience much stress. In the second column, list the things that make you unhappy or over which you feel considerable stress. Look back over the list of things that cause you stress and ask yourself these questions: *Which of these things can I control? Which of these things are out of my control?*

Evening Reflections

Look back over your list of things that cause you stress and are out of your control. My friend Jackie feels very responsible for her married daughter's happiness. Now while it is true that Jackie can certainly be involved in her daughter's happiness, is it in her control whether her daughter is happy or not? Doesn't her daughter have to take control of her own happiness? The point is, we may be creating a lot of stress in our lives by trying to be in control of things that simply are not in our control. Think about one thing that is causing stress in your life that is not really in your control. Ask for God's help in releasing control of that stressful situation.

What we *can* be in control of is our own life, our daily choices, our thoughts, our faith, our words, and our actions. Ask for God's help in accepting control over these things.

Reflect on Philippians 2:13: "For it is God who is at work in you, enabling you both to will and to work for his good pleasure."

Section 4 Chapter 23

Adventurous Living

The LORD is my light and my salvation; / whom shall I fear? / The LORD is the stronghold of my life; / of whom shall I be afraid?

(Psalm 27:1)

I recently took up bicycling. I am in my midlife years and had never been inclined to regress to my childhood behavior of riding a bike. My grown-up, common-sense mind cautioned me against biking. "What if I tip over?" "I don't know how to fix a flat tire, and I don't want to know how." "Biking makes my rear end hurt." And so the excuses went.

However, we all know that strange things happen to our minds (and our bodies) during midlife. So when my friend Naomi asked me to come with her on a week-long, five hundred mile bicycle ride along the Wisconsin River, I disregarded my mature-minded thinking and decided to go for it. This would mean taking some risk, making some choices, taking some chances. I remembered the words of Grace Hopper, "A ship in port is safe, but that's not what ships are built for." I needed a physical challenge. I needed to know my limits. I needed an adventure.

Did I tip over? Yes. Can I fix a flat tire? You bettcha. Did I jump out of my seat when I ran over a snake? Uh-huh. Did my rear end hurt? Let's just say, I'm still in my rear-end recovery program. Did I make it? YES I DID! As Helen Keller once said, "Life is either a daring adventure or it is nothing."

I recently read a study that asked people what they most

regretted in their lives. In other words, if they had their life to live again, what would they do differently? The study reported that people end up having two kinds of regrets. The authors called them "hot" regrets and "wistful" regrets.

Hot regret is the quick anger felt after discovering that you have made a mistake, like locking the keys in the car. We all know the feeling.

Wistful regret, on the other hand, comes from a longer range view. It is the sad feeling that life might have been better if only we had taken certain actions. Asked to describe their biggest regrets, participants in this study most often cited things they had failed to do. They did not regret what they tried to do, even when they failed to accomplish their goals. They regretted that they had failed to try; failed to seize the moment; failed to go for it.

To feel less stressed and to truly enjoy life we must occasionally push ourselves out of our comfort zone. This is what energizes us and helps make life an exhilarating adventure. The bicycle trip was a true adventure for me. I would have felt wistful regret had I not given it a try. I would have missed the morning mist coming off the lake, seeing and hearing the sandhill cranes, the exhilaration of coasting downhill faster than I ever had before, biking in a downpour (even the cows had enough sense to get out of the rain), the eagle soaring overhead, the company of wonderful adventurous people, and a feeling of absolute exhilaration at being out in God's beautiful world.

Some of life's greatest stress is a result of regret, of being afraid to stretch ourselves for fear of failure. Fear of failure—have you ever just given up on a hope, a dream, a goal, an adventure because you were afraid of failing? Reflect on 2 Timothy 1:7: "For God did not give us a spirit of cowardice, but rather a spirit of power and of love and of self-discipline."

Fear can be absolutely incapacitating. Think about this definition of fear:

False
Evidence
Appearing
Real

I find this English proverb helpful: "Fear knocked at the door. Faith answered. Nobody was there."

Accepting the challenge to grow, to try new things, and even to learn from tough times is a challenge that can bring greater happiness and fulfillment to your life. Sometimes we choose our challenges, like my bike ride, but sometimes great challenges come our way without our choosing. I am thinking of challenges such as dealing with the death of a loved one, loss of a job, personal or family illness. Learning how to grow and learn from these challenges is a quality that stress less people have developed. Bruce Laingen, former charge d'affaires for the American Embassy in Iran said, "Human beings are like tea bags. You don't know your strength until you're put in hot water."

Do you see life as an adventure? Do you seek opportunities to stretch and grow? Are you willing to put aside your fear of failure and test your limits? Are you able to face the unexpected challenges that come your way with power and love and self-discipline? Feeling like you are stuck in a rut and living a life of drudgery can be very stressful. You have a choice. You can choose adventurous living or you can choose drudgery. What will it be?

Message to Remember

The second key to stress less living is living with a sense of adventure. Dare to try new things, to overcome fear of failure and to stretch yourself. You will add joy and adventure to your life.

Start Today

Confide in one person an adventure that you would like to take.

Prepare for the next chapter by completing "How Stress Resistant Are You?" at the end of the chapter.

Evening Reflections

Reminisce about a time when you felt alive and invigorated. What were you doing? What was it about that experience that made you feel so alive?

Think more about an adventure that would excite and challenge you. Begin to plan how you can accomplish this adventure. Be realistic, but challenge yourself to stretch and grow.

God came that we might have life and have it abundantly. Think about this.

"Do not fear, for I am with you, / do not be afraid, for I am your God; / I will strengthen you, I will help you, / I will uphold you with my victorious right hand" (Isaiah 41:10)

How Stress-Resistant Are You?

This quiz gives you an idea of how resistant you are to stress, or how vulnerable. Rate each item on the test from 1 (almost always) to 5 (never), according to how the statement pertains to you. Mark each item, even if it does not apply to you (for instance, if you do not smoke, give yourself a 1, not a 0). Add up your score.

If your total is 45 or below, you probably have excellent resistance to stress. A score over 45 indicates some vulnerability to stress, and a score over 55 indicates serious vulnerability to stress.

1 2 3 4 5   1. I eat at least one hot, balanced meal a day.

1 2 3 4 5   2. I get seven to eight hours of sleep at least four nights a week.

1 2 3 4 5   3. I give and receive affection regularly.

1 2 3 4 5   4. I have at least one relative within 50 miles of home on whom I can rely.

1 2 3 4 5   5. I exercise to the point of perspiration at least twice weekly.

1 2 3 4 5   6. I limit myself to less than half a pack of cigarettes a day.

1 2 3 4 5   7. I take fewer than five alcoholic drinks a week.

1 2 3 4 5   8. I am the appropriate weight for my height and build.

1 2 3 4 5   9. My income covers my basic expenses.

1 2 3 4 5 10. I get strength from my religious beliefs.

1 2 3 4 5 11. I regularly attend social activities.

1 2 3 4 5 12. I have a network of close friends and acquaintances.

1 2 3 4 5 13. I have one or more friends to confide in about personal matters.

1 2 3 4 5 14. I am in good health (including eyesight, hearing, teeth).

1 2 3 4 5 15. I am able to speak openly about feelings when angry or worried.

1 2 3 4 5 16. I discuss domestic problems—like chores and money—with the members of my household.

1 2 3 4 5 17. I have fun at least once a week.

1 2 3 4 5 18. I can organize my time effectively.

1 2 3 4 5 19. I drink fewer than three cups of coffee (or other caffeine-rich beverages) a day.

1 2 3 4 5 20. I take some quiet time for myself during the day.

Total Score = _____

(Developed by psychologists Lyle H. Miller and Alma Dell Smith of Boston University Medical Center)

HEALTHY LIVING

Whether you eat or drink, or whatever you do, do everything for the glory of God. (1 Corinthians 10:31)

Stress is an emotional and physical reaction, and developing a healthier than average attitude and lifestyle can help you be a better than average stress manager. A healthy lifestyle—exercising, eating right, not smoking or drinking, and getting enough rest and relaxation—can reduce your chances of getting stress-related illness and help you feel better about yourself. In this chapter we will look at tips for maintaining a healthy and positive lifestyle with special emphasis on the relationship between nutrition and stress.

The assessment test, "How Stress Resistant Are You?" on the previous page allows you to analyze your lifestyle habits. Look back over your answers. How stress resistant are you?

Exercise

In section three you learned that aerobic exercises and stretching exercises are especially effective techniques for stress reduction. Aerobic exercise helps your body use oxygen more efficiently; it strengthens your heart and lungs and helps dissipate excess stress hormones. Stretching exercises help relieve tense muscles and improve your overall flexibility. A regular exercise program is an essential part of a healthy lifestyle.

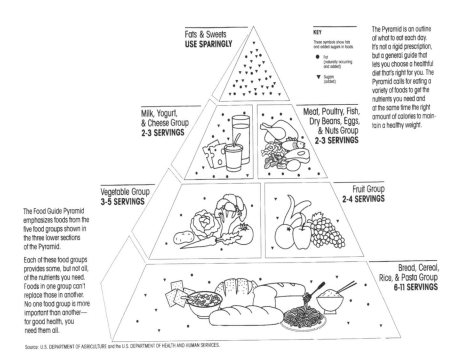

Fats & Sweets
USE SPARINGLY

KEY

These symbols show fats and added sugars in foods

● Fat (naturally occurring and added)

▼ Sugars (added)

The Pyramid is an outline of what to eat each day. It's not a rigid prescription, but a general guide that lets you choose a healthful diet that's right for you. The Pyramid calls for eating a variety of foods to get the nutrients you need and at the same time the right amount of calories to maintain a healthy weight.

Milk, Yogurt, & Cheese Group
2-3 SERVINGS

Meat, Poultry, Fish, Dry Beans, Eggs, & Nuts Group
2-3 SERVINGS

Vegetable Group
3-5 SERVINGS

Fruit Group
2-4 SERVINGS

The Food Guide Pyramid emphasizes foods from the five food groups shown in the three lower sections of the Pyramid.

Each of these food groups provides some, but not all, of the nutrients you need. Foods in one group can't replace those in another. No one food group is more important than another—for good health, you need them all.

Bread, Cereal, Rice, & Pasta Group
6-11 SERVINGS

Source: U.S. DEPARTMENT OF AGRICULTURE and the U.S. DEPARTMENT OF HEALTH AND HUMAN SERVICES.

Nutrition

For good health eat a balanced diet. Follow the guidelines in the Food Guide Pyramid above. But what does food have to do with stress? We will focus on two important aspects of nutrition and stress. First, the relationship between food and our emotions and, second, nutritional factors associated with stress.

Food as a Pacifier

Raise your hand if you eat only to meet your nutritional needs and only when you are hungry. Not many hands going up, I see! It comes as no surprise that many of us eat for emotional reasons, such as when we are stressed. While eating can have a calming effect, use caution to avoid abusing food as a coping technique.

Obesity and over-consumption are growing health problems in this country. The danger is in using food as a tranquilizer to calm our hearts and minds rather than finding constructive ways to manage emotional issues such as anger, guilt, boredom, loneliness, lack of meaning and purpose, or anxiety. As our society becomes increasingly obese, we must remember that the problem is more than over-consumption; there are underlying emotional issues contributing to the problem. Eating disorders like anorexia, bulimia, and overeating are clearly related to stress and an individual's ability to cope with stressors in a healthy manner.

While you may not have an eating disorder, it is still very helpful to think about your eating habits and how they relate to your emotions. Using food to relieve stress on a regular basis is not a healthy stress-relief practice.

This is not to say that you can not find joy and pleasure in eating. I must admit (lest I be thought a hypocrite by any of you who know me), I have been known to head straight for my private stash of chocolate when I am feeling stressed. (There is a reason why *desserts* is *stressed* spelled backwards). I keep little emergency chocolate supplies hidden in strategic locations—the back of my desk drawer at work, in a bowl on the top shelf of the cupboard, under my car seat. Our kids even tell of finding chocolate covered peanuts hidden in our broken dishwasher. Is this bad? Let me just say that I am a great believer in the "all things in moderation" idea. I also think I personally would be more stressed by depriving myself of chocolate than by allowing for occasional indulgences.

The point is, food can be used as a way of stuffing your emotions resulting in some very unhealthy consequences. Learn to enjoy food but do not use food to avoid dealing with emotional issues.

NUTRITION AND STRESS

Below are some additional tips based on the relationship between stress and nutrition:

- **Eat a healthy breakfast.** Stress increases the production of certain stress hormones that are thought to be responsible for craving carbohydrate-rich foods, especially sweets. Eating a healthy breakfast is believed to help maintain and keep in balance levels of the chemicals responsible for these cravings.
- **Limit simple sugars.** An excess of simple sugars tends to

deplete vitamin stores, especially B-complex vitamins. Depleted vitamin levels can result in fatigue, irritability, and anxiety. Additionally, excess amounts of simple sugars may cause changes in your blood sugar (glucose) levels resulting in feelings of fatigue, headache, and irritability.

- **Limit caffeine.** Caffeine is a stimulant that is quickly absorbed in the blood with a direct effect on the brain. A chemical stimulant in caffeine produces amphetamine-like characteristics. The result is a heightened state of alertness, which may make you more susceptible to perceived stress. Caffeine is also a diuretic and can result in the loss of minerals such as calcium and magnesium.

- **Avoid the caffeine/sugar crash.** You can become dependent on sugar or caffeine to get a surge of energy. The problem is when the immediate effects wear off, you discover you have only borrowed the energy—from yourself. First comes the high, then the crash, leaving you drained and stressed.

- **Limit alcohol.** Consuming excessive amounts of alcohol can deplete your body of water-soluble vitamins and minerals resulting in a weakened immune system that makes you more susceptible to illness. Many nutritionists suggest that more than one drink per day is excessive. Alcohol is also a depressant and can have a major impact on your ability to deal with life stressors in a healthy manner.

Limiting your use of sugar, caffeine, and alcohol are important for promoting good health and reducing stress.

- **Manage stress.** Chronic stress can deplete several important vitamins that affect mental alertness and thus result in depression and insomnia. Stress also is associated with depletion of calcium and the inability of bones to absorb calcium properly. This can set the stage for osteoporosis.

Avoid Unhealthy Habits

You all know people (you may be one yourself) who turn to unhealthy behaviors as a way of coping with too much stress. Habits like smoking, drinking, and illegal drugs can initially make a person feel more relaxed. As you all know, these temporary fixes only add to a person's stress over time. You have a choice. You can choose alcohol to try to escape from dealing with stressors or you can choose to deal with the stressor—to learn and grow as a child of God.

Message to Remember

Maintaining an overall healthy lifestyle is important to stress less living. Exercise, nutrition, rest, and dealing constructively with stressors rather than masking them with unhealthy habits contribute to your health and wellness.

Start Today

Complete the Daily Food Diary on page 114. You may want to make several copies of this page and maintain a record over several days to get a better pattern of your eating.

Include the following:

1. **Time of day**—Enter the time that you are eating the food.
2. **Place**—Enter the location where you are eating. For example, kitchen, car, sitting in the recliner, at the bar.
3. **Associated activity**—What else were you doing while you were eating? For example, watching TV, reading the paper, driving to work, fixing supper, visiting with friends.
4. **Reason/Mood**—What made you want to eat what you did? What were your emotions, thoughts, and feelings while you were eating?
5. **Food and amount**—Do your best to record everything you eat. If, for example, you eat a Big Mac, record "two all beef patties, special sauce, lettuce, cheese, pickles, onions, on a sesame seed bun."
6. **Food category**—Put a check under the Food Guide Pyramid food group where the food belongs.
7. **Water**—Remember, choose to drink eight glasses of water each day.

Evening Reflections

Look back over your Daily Food Diary. Do you often eat for emotional reasons? Can you identify some specific feelings that are related to the times you eat when you are not necessarily hungry? Overeaters Anonymous uses HALT to remind us of four feelings that frequently lead to overeating:

Hungry, Angry, Lonely, and Tired.

Write down one thing you will do on a regular basis to improve your nutrition.

Think about the scripture, Galatians 6:9: "So let us not grow weary in doing what is right, for we will reap at harvest-time, if we do not give up."

DAILY FOOD DIARY

DATE	(1) Time of Day	(2) Place	(3) Associated Activity	(4) Reason/Mood	(5) Food and Amount	(6) Food Group						(7) Water
						DAY M TU W TH F SA SU						
						#1 Bread	#2 Veggie	#3 Fruit	#4 Dairy	#5 Meat	#6 Fats/Sweets	

Section 4 Chapter 25

$\mathcal{S}$OLITUDE

The apostles gathered around Jesus, and told him all that they had done and taught. He said to them, "Come away to a deserted place all by yourselves and rest a while." For many were coming and going, and they had no leisure even to eat. (Mark 6:30-31)

Arranging time for solitude is an essential ingredient of a stress less life. Stress less people take time out—I call it solo time. They plan their life to allow time to escape to a quiet place.

Solitude is the experience of being by yourself without feeling lonely or alone. Many of you are constantly surrounded by people. Read today's scripture again. Sound familiar? Many were coming and going. No leisure even to eat. When was the last time you spent a day or two completely alone for the sole purpose of self-renewal? Taking time to retreat from your daily routine allows you to connect with yourself and with God in a powerful way. You can immerse yourself in the moment, free from the distractions of everyday life. You will find freedom in your thoughts and actions that will surprise and delight you. Solitude, by choice and at the right times, can help you sort through what is on your heart and mind. A retreat can leave you feeling refreshed, rejuvenated, and spiritually invigorated.

A couple of years ago I started taking a day off each season. I always end up out in nature. We live in the beautiful Black Hills of South Dakota so I am lucky to enjoy hikes in the autumn, cross country skiing in the winter, swimming in mountain lakes in the summer, and long cool bike rides in the spring. But mostly on my days off I just walk, sit, think and *be* instead of *do*.

Not long ago, I spent one of my days off at Devil's Tower in nearby Wyoming. In 1906, President Teddy Roosevelt designated Devil's Tower as the nation's first natural monument. Just to see and experience this amazing natural wonder brings a spiritual awakening.

Devil's Tower National Monument—The Legend

"One day an Indian tribe was camped beside a river and seven small girls were playing at a distance. The region had a large bear population and a bear began to chase the girls. They ran back toward their village, but the bear was about to catch them. The girls jumped upon a rock about three feet high and began to pray to the rock, 'Rock, take pity on us; Rock, save us.' The rock heard the pleas of the young girls and began to elongate itself upwards, pushing them higher and higher out of reach of the bear. The bear clawed and jumped at the sides of the rock, and broke its claws and fell to the ground. The bear continued to jump at the rock until the girls were pushed up into the sky, where they are to this day in a group of seven little stars (the Pleiades). The marks of the bear claws are there yet. As one looks upon the tower and contemplates its uniqueness, it isn't hard to imagine this legend as a fact."

I sat for several hours on this rainy spring day at the base of the 865-foot-high monument. The rocks and boulders around the base of the tower are actually broken pieces of columns that fell from the sides. I thought about the legend of the tower. I thought about the Native Americans who many years ago, and even yet today, come to sit at this magnificent rock.

It was a truly spiritual experience to sit at the base of this amazing natural wonder and reflect on the generations before me who came here, just like me, to ponder the purpose and meaning of life.

In this most natural of environments, God's creation, I felt connected to life in a way that is hard to explain.

Finding time for this kind of spiritual retreat is important. Sometimes we need to get away from it all. The challenge is incorporating the peace and serenity you discover into your daily life. In between your spiritual retreats, make the most of a quiet evening alone. Wrap yourself in your coziest bathrobe, cook a pot of soup, put on some music, and relax. Make an appointment with yourself for pampering. You can make a decision to live a life that allows for this sustenance on a regular basis.

Think about how you can make time to be restored and refreshed. Think about solitude as time for re-creation. This anonymous poem reminds us of the importance of taking time for ourselves.

If you keep your nose to the grindstone rough,
And you keep it down there long enough,
In time you'll say there's no such thing
As brooks that babble and birds that sing.
These three will all your world compose:
Just you, the stone, and your poor old nose.

Message to Remember

Taking time to "get away from it all" is the fourth key to stress less living.

Start Today

Make a plan for a day off. Think about where you will go and what you will do. This is an entire day that you spend alone and away from home. Plan to spend the night. Try to arrange for at least part of the day to be out in nature.

Evening Reflections

"Be still before the LORD, and wait patiently for him; / do not fret over those who prosper in their way, / over those who carry out evil devices" (Psalm 37:7).

How do you feel about your plan to have a day off? I suspect some of you are busy thinking about reasons why you simply *cannot* take an entire day for yourself. Yes, you can. No matter how busy you are, no matter how many people are depending on you, no matter how important the work that you do is, you can take a day off, *if you decide to*. Take a sick day from work (I wish we had health days to take off occasionally, just to stay healthy). Before you go to bed tonight, decide on the day that you will take off and start making those plans. Write it on your calender. Let you family know you will be out of touch that day. Make whatever arrangements you need—just do it!

Section 4 Chapter 26

*J*OYFUL LIVING

A cheerful heart is a good medicine, / but a downcast spirit dries up the bones. (Proverbs 17:22)

*H*ow can you use humor and laughter to manage stress in your life and enhance the quality of each day? Studies show that humor promotes mental, emotional, physical, and spiritual well-being. There is a strong relationship between good humor and good health. Laughter results in the release of endorphins, natural mood-lifters, and helps restore physiological homeostasis.

Laughter not only feels good but it is good for you. The late Dr. Norman Cousins found that ten minutes of laughter allowed two hours of pain-free sleep. He promoted the idea that if negative thoughts can result in illness and disease, then positive thoughts should enhance health. He called laughter "internal jogging."

The idea that laughter is good medicine was never presented to me more powerfully than in the stress story written by one of my nursing students, Amy Porath. Amy consented to let me share her touching story with you:

I got married when I was eighteen. My husband was twenty. We made plans like so many newly married couples make . . . careers, buying a house, starting a family. Two short years into our marriage our dreams were shattered. I was three months pregnant when we learned that my husband had brain cancer. His prognosis was extremely poor and I was told that he probably would not live to see our baby born.

This was not acceptable to my husband. He told me that he was going to live...not only long enough to see the birth, but long enough so his child would get to know him and be able to remember him. Thus our battle began. It was not only a battle with the cancer, but with the medical professionals who told us that he had only six months to live.

I started reading books to him in his hospital bed, oftentimes not knowing if he could even hear me. I found compilations of funny stories and jokes. I would laugh—most of the times so I would not cry. Then came the day when he laughed with me. He became alert and oriented and ready to take on each day with a smile. He became the talk of the hospital unit. The staff were amazed at his progress and commented that he always had a smile on his face. He was always good for a joke.

Our daughter was born in March of 1987. My husband was by my side. He was there on her first day of preschool, kindergarten, first grade and second grade.

It has been almost four years since my husband passed away. It was not until he died that I could fully see his strength and lust for life. The stress that I felt knowing that I was going to lose my husband surely must have been outmatched by the stress he must have had knowing that he was the one who was going to die. He never showed it...which is what helped me cope throughout his illness. His strength and sense of humor carried us both. I thank him for that. I thank him for not giving up and having the courage to laugh at his six-month prognosis. I thank him for showing me that life is not just black and white. I thank him for helping me put things into perspective. I thank him for teaching me that laughter is good medicine. I thank him for laughing his way into our daughter's life.

If you ask our daughter, she'll say, "My daddy was a funny man."

Does it sometimes seem like there is an unwritten rule that we as Christians don't dare be too happy? After all, life is serious business. There is sadness and suffering all around. Somehow if we dare to be happy we think it diminishes the seriousness of the pain around us. We need to collectively change our thinking. By being joyful, you are able to spread joy to others; by being happy, you are able to spread happiness to others; by being able to love, you are able to spread love to others. Just ask Amy and her daughter.

Message to Remember

Seeing and experiencing the joy in life is a key to stress less living. We can experience happiness and laughter even during the tough times.

Start Today

Thank and praise God for being with you and walking beside you this day. Keep a list today of specific things, people, and events you are thankful for—no matter how big or small.

Think about God's word in John 15:10-11: "If you keep my commandments, you will abide in my love, just as I have kept my Father's commandments and abide in his love. I have said these things to you so that my joy may be in you, and that your joy may be complete."

Evening Reflections

Think about Habakkuk 3: 17-19: "Though the fig tree does not blossom, / and no fruit is on the vines; / though the produce of the olive fails / and the fields yield no food; / though the flock is cut off from the fold / and there is no herd in the stalls, / yet I will rejoice in the LORD; / I will exalt in the God of my salvation. / GOD, the Lord, is my strength; / he makes my feet like the feet of a deer, / and makes me tread upon the heights." How does this scripture reading relate to your life?

The average person laughs about fifteen times a day. How do you compare? How often do you have a good old belly laugh? You know, the kind that brings tears running down your cheeks and leaves you feeling a little out of control.

Reflect on these words as you prepare for sleep, Isaiah 55:12: "For you shall go out in joy, / and be led back in peace; / the mountains and the hills before you / shall burst into song, / and all the trees of the field shall clap their hands."

*C*LEAR PRIORITIES

Humble yourselves therefore under the mighty hand of God, so that he may exalt you in due time. Cast all your anxiety on him, because he cares for you. (I Peter 5:6-7)

We hear a lot these days about not having enough time. This gives us the impression that somehow some people got more of the stuff than others—it's just not so. When it comes to time, we are all treated equally. How many hours were in your day yesterday? Do you know anyone that had more than twenty-four hours in their day, or seven days in their week, or fifty-two weeks in their year?

So the real issue is not how much time you have, it is how you choose to use your time. For many that means packing our days from morning to night with important things to do. Every day you make dozens of decisions and choices about how you will spend your time. These choices directly affect your stress level. Today we will look at how you can manage time rather than letting time manage you—an important idea for a less stressed you.

I have to confess to you that the first draft of this chapter was very different than the final draft. I started out detailing a rather elaborate time management system complete with goal statements for all major areas of your life, completion dates, purpose statement, to do lists, and on and on. Then one day I was thumbing through a magazine when an advertisement for a daily planner caught my eye. A young man, his pretty wife, and cute baby were sitting on the beach looking very happy and relaxed. The caption read, "Oddly enough, getting your schedule straight helps you keep your priorities straight. "

I read the caption a couple of times and it just was not right. Organizing your time does not make your priorities right. You have to *first* determine your priorities and then plan your time. Big deal, you say, but this was an amazing insight to me. People a lot smarter than you and me have not figured this out. We expend a lot of time and stress trying to get our schedules organized, yet if we do not have clear priotities to guide us, will we ever feel satisfied?

It is like putting together a puzzle and discovering that the pieces are not all there. No matter how much time you spend rearranging the pieces, you are not going to get the outcome you want—a completed picture. Our family recently completed a 2,000 piece puzzle and at the end there was one piece missing. I cannot tell you the stress and frustration that caused me. The puzzle remained on the dining room table for several days. The project was not complete without the missing piece. (You will be happy to know that the missing piece was found in the basement. We think our cat Pepe had something to do with that.)

Trying to schedule your time when your priorities are unclear is like putting together a puzzle when pieces are missing. You must first step back to consider the bigger picture. The key is not prioritizing your schedule. It is scheduling your priorities. The question is, *What really matters to you?*

OK, that's not too hard. You just need to start with what is really important and plan your time to allow for these things. If you are like me, the first big question is, "Hmmm, let's see now, what really does matter to me?" The first things that came to my mind were my family, my spiritual health, and my physical health. No surprises there. The next step was to evaluate if I was spending my time on those things that really were most important to me. This was an amazing eye-opener to me. I took out my always with me schedule book and looked back over the past week's activities.

Like many of you, my job consumed a big chunk of time. I

spent over 40 hours last week at my job as nursing faculty at a university. While I really love teaching, I could not help but notice that last week I spent six hours in committee meetings, which I do not love. I also spent about seven hours commuting to my job.

Then I looked at my evenings. Jim and I have always tried to keep our evenings open for family time. Much to my dismay, I saw that in the last week I had only two evenings out of seven at home. Well, yes, but all those things I was doing were important, I justify—teaching an evening class, an important meeting at church to organize a parish nurse program, participating in a twenty-four-hour cancer walk, etc.

Well, you get the idea. When we look honestly at our hectic lifestyle, we may find that we are not spending our time on what really is most important to us. What I found was that even though many of the things I was doing were in my mind good and important things, this was not necessarily the best way for me to spend my time. For inner and outer peace, and to nourish my soul, I needed to make some changes.

Never before in history have we been able to do more, have more, go more places, and see more things. We have worn ourselves out trying to have it all and do it all.

Rest and Relaxation

Remember that sometimes the best thing you can do for yourself is nothing at all. You know that relaxation is important to managing stress, so do not pack your days with endless chores. Plan time to relax and to enjoy some free time. Your body needs sleep to refresh itself, especially when you are under stress.

You might want to think back to the story of the creation: "And on the seventh day God finished the work that he had done, and he rested on the seventh day from all the work that he had done. So God blessed the seventh day and hallowed it, because on it God rested from all the work that he had done in creation" (Genesis 2:2-3). Consider that if God took time to rest, you can too.

Judy, a university instructor, and her husband Carl, a minister, appeared to be living the good life. They had worked hard to build a big, beautiful home with a beautifully landscaped yard. At lunch Judy shared with me that they had decided to sell their house and simplify their life. She explained that much of their time was put into maintaining their house and the mortgage payments were a constant stressor. Additionally, Judy felt obligated to make their home available for many church functions. Judy said, "Even though I'm spending more and more time on church activities, I'm beginning to feel spiritually drained."

Priorities

So the first step in managing your time for less stress is to get your priorities straight. Remember, if you do not decide how to spend your day, someone else will decide for you. We frequently allow the *urgent* to take precedence over the *important*. We demand endless energy and activity of ourselves. This tremendous pressure and the rushing of over-activity can cause you to lose sight of what is really important. So what are the priorities? This is no secret. Jesus told us: "But strive first for the kingdom of God and his righteousness, and all these things will be given to you as well" (Matthew 6:33).

What are the priorities in your life? Money? Health? Family? Climbing the corporate ladder? It is not that these things are necessarily bad, but if your first priority is anything but the kingdom of God and his righteousness, things will be out of balance for you. By putting God's priorities first, everything else will be clear to you. What are you seeking *first* in your life?

Message to Remember

Stress less people know their priorities. They plan their schedule for what is most important.

Start Today

Think back over the chapters in this book. Pick out the three chapters that seemed to most speak to you. What were the messages from these chapters that you want to be sure to remember and apply in your life?

Write a short paragraph about what it means to have God guiding your life.

Evening Reflections

Read the Bible story about the wise man who built his house upon the rock.

"Everyone then who hears these words of mine and acts on them will be like a wise man who built his house on rock. The rain fell, the floods came, and the winds blew and beat on that house, but it did not fall, because it had been founded on rock. And everyone who hears these words of mine and does not act on them will be like a foolish man who built his house on sand. The rain fell, and the floods came, and the winds blew and beat against that house, and it fell—and great was its fall!" (Matthew 7:24-27).

Think about how this relates to your life. Is your life built on God's solid foundation? When the storms in life come, as they most certainly will, will you stand or fall? Think about what needs to happen in your life to assure that your foundation is firm. What is truly important to you?

Think back over the past week. Focus on how you spent your time. Are you using your time on what is most important to you? Write down your two or three top priorities. If a time management expert evaluated your schedule for last week based on your priorities, what would he or she find? Are you spending your time on your priorities? Write down one specific time waster. Replace that time with one specific thing that is truly important to you. Remember, you do have a choice.

Section 4 Chapter 28

$\mathscr{L}$OVE YOURSELF

By contrast, the fruit of the Spirit is love, joy, peace, patience, kindness, generosity, faithfulness, gentleness, and self-control. There is no law against such things. (Galatians 5:22-23)

*T*hink back over the seven keys to stress less living: balanced control, healthy living, adventurous living, solitude, joyful living, clear priorities, and loving yourself. After I had written the chapters for section four, I thought about today's scripture and could not help but notice that many of the keys to stress less living relate closely to the fruits of the spirit. Coincidence? I don't think so. The keys to a more balanced, whole, healthy life are directly connected to your spiritual vitality.

This is the last chapter in *Stress Less*, and it is the first chapter in a lifetime of more abundant living for you. Develop a plan to guide you. As you plan for your future, think of the person you want to be in five, ten, or twenty years. Picture how you want your life to be, your energy level, your physical, emotional, and spiritual health. Think about the people in your life and the wonderful gift you give them by caring for yourself today and in the days to come.

There is no single strategy or plan for managing stress that will work for everyone. You each have different stressors, different responses to stressors, and different strategies that work for you. The most important elements in success are knowing yourself and listening to yourself. With an open heart and mind, God will work in you. Remember the formula, God plus people (you) equals accomplishment. Pay attention to the emotions and thoughts that accompany your stress response and take charge of handling stress in a healthy way. Know your inner resources that will help you live more abundantly.

Look at the Stress Less Contract at the end of this chapter. Think about these things as you develop your plan for healthy living:

1. Identify Your Stressors

Before you can manage stressors you must clearly identify them. Use the various assessment tests you have completed to help you identify the stressors in your life. Your stress journal from chapter nine will help you spot some patterns.

2. Design Your Program

You have learned many different techniques for combating stress. Choose the techniques that work best for you and create an action plan for change. Complete the Stress Less Contract. Think about these things:

—Include *specific* behaviors. Be realistic. Ease in to change. Think about lifestyle habits rather than temporary fixes. For example, you might be willing and able to exercise for an hour each day for a couple weeks, but can you maintain that habit? You will receive greater benefits from exercising twenty minutes four days a week on a long-term basis than exercising one hour each day on a short-term basis. Think about lifestyle habits rather than temporary change.

—Remember that healthy living is an important aspect of managing stress, so include some behaviors to enhance your overall health.

—Review and revise your plan on a regular basis. Pick a certain date each month to review your plan. You will want to make changes.

—Be sure to plan for rewards. If you faithfully practice your deep breathing exercises, you might reward yourself with a leisurely bubble bath or an hour of relaxing reading at the end of the day. The idea is to make this a very positive and rewarding experience. Think of your stress plan as a gift you are giving yourself rather than one more thing to do.

3. Getting Help

There may be times in your life when the techniques and ideas presented here are not enough. Our capacities for self-healing have limitations. There are times when our needs exceed our ability to cope and we require outside help. Find out where and when to go for help when you need additional support.

I would like to conclude *Stress Less* by sharing a personal story. My quest for a more abundant and joy-filled life comes in part from these experiences. They greatly influenced my desire to write *Stress Less*.

It is probably an understatement to say I have had several close calls in my life—times when my life could have ended. A friend once told me I was like a cat with nine lives. It started early. Growing up on a farm with my twin sisters Pat and Peg and my brother Monte was a constant adventure. When I was a child, Monte decided some horse medicine would make me feel better. **Thank God**, *we got to the hospital in time for a stomach pumping. Then there was the time I got run over by a tractor. That is a story in itself.* **Thank God**, *my young bones were pliable and the ground was soft from a recent rain.*

As a teen, I was in a rather serious school bus accident, but came through with only some bumps and bruises. The trend continued in my young adult years when I survived a parachuting accident. To this day my survival remains a mystery. (I don't even want to know what you're thinking.) **Thank God**, *for protecting me.*

A few years ago I was flying home from some meetings. We were a couple of thousand feet up in the air when we heard crackling and popping noises and, suddenly, the emergency exit door on the small airplane flew off. The cold air rushed in and the noise was so deafening we couldn't hear one another. **Thank God**, *the pilot was able to turn the plane around and get us safely back on ground. That was a frightening experience!*

Then last year I was diagnosed with malignant melanoma, which, **thank God**, *we think we caught early enough that the cancerous cells* *hadn't spread. I believe it was more than a coincidence that I had gone to the doctor for something else and rather casually mentioned the mole on the back of my leg. Our daughter, Jenny, had noticed the mole several months earlier and said it looked "funny." When the doctor told me the mole was cancerous his words hit me hard. He said, "Call your daughter and tell her she saved your life." Once again, I was reminded of my mortality and reminded to* **thank God** *for watching over me.*

I believe I am alive today for a reason. These experiences all have changed me and given me a real appreciation for each day I have. We never know when we wake up in the morning if this day will be our last. I have faced my own mortality profoundly. This has caused me to want to make a difference during the time I have on this earth.

My prayer for you is that as a child of God you will know that you can live an abundant, joyful life. Thank you for letting me walk with you on your journey to more abundant living.

Message to Remember
Your plan for continuing your journey to more abundant and stress less living is the key to the long term benefits. Make your journey a pleasant and joy-filled one.

Start Today
Complete your Stress Less Contract.

Evening Reflections
Do you believe you are here for a reason? Think about some things that have happened in your life that have shaped how you view your meaning and purpose in life.

Reflect back on the previous chapters. Think about how you have come to know yourself better and become more aware of the factors that influence your life. Thank God for the opportunity to learn and grow as a child of God.

Write down the two most important things you have learned from *Stress Less.*

Read and reflect on *Be Good to You*.

Be Good to You
Be yourself—truthfully
Accept yourself—gratefully
Value yourself—joyfully
Forgive yourself—completely
Treat yourself—generously
Balance yourself—harmoniously
Bless yourself—abundantly
Trust yourself—confidently
Love yourself—wholeheartedly
Empower yourself—prayerfully
Give yourself—enthusiastically
Express yourself—radiantly

Source unknown

Think about how you can *be good to you*.

Stress Less Contract of Commitment

I, _____, understand the effects of stress on my health. I commit to incorporating the following behaviors into my daily routine to help manage stress:

1. _____

_____

2. _____

_____

3. _____

_____

4. _____

_____

I will begin my program on _____. I will add one behavior _____, moving on to the next behavior once the earlier one(s) are firmly established as habits.

I will reward myself at least once during each week that I successfully stay with my program by _____

_____

_____   _____
(Your signature)   (Date)

_____
(Witness)

Dear Reader,

Today, as I rode my bike up Spearfish Canyon, I heard the geese overhead. The air was chilly and fresh. The leaves were a bright golden yellow and the hills were spotted with patches of sparkling snow from an early storm. I was reminded that last fall Stress Less *was just a vague idea in the back of my mind.*

Writing Stress Less *has been an adventure for me. I have learned and grown from this experience. One of the ways that my life has been changed is that I am more deliberate in enjoying the moment. I believe we miss many of God's miracles that happen around us every day because we are so busy "doing." I have learned to be better at "being."*

Thank you for coming with me on this leg of our journey to more abundant living. I am filled with thanks for the many people, including you, who have joined me on the journey. My prayers are with you as you continue on your quest for a stress less life.

I want to leave you with one of my favorite reminders of the beauty that is ours today.

Ten thousand flowers in spring,
    the moon in autumn,
a cool breeze in summer,
    snow in the winter.
If your mind is not clouded by unnecessary things,
this is the best season of your life.
            (Wu-men—12th century Chinese scholar)

Enjoy this moment. Enjoy this day. Feel peaceful. Feel blessed. Let this be the best season of your life.

Health and happiness,

Margie

The Stress Less Group Guide

Some of you will use *Stress Less* as a short-term study. This is a great idea! The support, fun, fellowship, and new perspectives of the group will help make the ideas come alive for you. This leader's guide will provide structure for your meetings and discussions.

First things first:
If your church or organization is offering *Stress Less* as a special program, then—

1. Designate a group leader. The group leader will
- Announce and promote the *Stress Less* study.
- Arrange for participants to sign up.
- Order books.
- Reserve a meeting place.
- Lead the weekly meetings.

NOTE: If you are studying *Stress Less* in your regular small group or Sunday school class, then you may decide to rotate leadership among the members of your class for the five-week period recommended for the study.

2. Decide when and where to meet. If possible, reserve at least one hour for each group session. If you study *Stress Less* during Sunday school, you will probably have less time, so plan carefully.

3. Decide on activities. The Group Guide contains more ideas and activities than you can do in a session. Plan to start and end on time. Choose the discussion questions and group activities that are most interesting and important to you.

4. Get involved. While the group leader can get things going, participants will benefit from active involvement. Encourage folk to sign up for the opening or closing devotion or to bring a healthy snack or to plan a Soul Soother activity.

5. Have fun. Enjoy the company and the new friends you will meet. Make this time together a time of wonderful Christian growth and fellowship.

Session One—Forming the Group

Use the first meeting to distribute the books and get acquainted with one another. I have included some discussion ideas and group activities. You will be meeting as a group five times including this session.

Group Activities and Discussion Ideas
• **Get acquainted.** Partner with someone you do not know. Spend a few minutes getting to know each other. Then introduce that person to the group.
Include in your discussion:
> One interesting thing about me or my life is ....
> The people around me know I am too stressed when ....

• **Discuss** why you decided to study *Stress Less*.

• **Choose Prayer Partners.** Put everyone's name and phone number in a hat and have each person draw a prayer partner. Your prayer partner will pray for you during the weeks to come. Prayer partners also may want to check in with each other during the week for support and encouragement.

• **Soul Soothers.** Each week do a Soul Soother together as a group. Choose from the list on the next page or, better yet, come up with some new ideas. Some of these take a little planning, so ask volunteers to plan for the next week. Someone might bring a soothing candle to a meeting or treat everyone to a cup of chamomile tea. Participants can give each other shoulder massages or someone might bring in the supplies so that each person can plant a flower to take home. Keep the Soul Soothers simple and be sure you choose something everyone in the group can do. Make it fun and relaxing.

• **For Next Week.**

Suggest that everyone read *Section One—Getting Started*, chapters 1 through 7, before the next meeting. Suggest that participants read one short chapter each day and spend a little time with the suggestions at the end of each chapter ("Start Today" and "Evening Reflections").

Soul Soothers

People tell me that these are the kinds of things they do to relax. Try some of them during the next four meetings. Let the group participants volunteer to share a Soul Soother from this list or bring in their own favorite.

Guided imagery	Get a manicure
Aroma therapy	Cry
Yoga	Meditate on scripture
Music	Clean a drawer
Prayer	Quiet meditation
Connect with nature	Read Psalm 23
Volunteer	Be out in nature
Warm bath with candles	Stretching exercises
Watch a movie	Laugh, have fun
Take a nap	Plants/Flowers
Stretch like a cat	Play with pets
Relax your jaw	Burn candles or incense
Sit in the dark and think of those who love you.	Talk with friends
Massage	Work in the garden
Journal writing	Play a game
Squeeze a stress ball	Fly a kite
Tae Kwon Do	Walk in the rain
Lifting weights	Read a poem
Exercise	Listen to a symphony
Dancing in the living room	Clean out a closet
Cup of chamomile tea	Memorize a Bible verse
	Breathe!

Session Two—Getting Started

Discussion Ideas

• Discuss as a group what you would *most* like to achieve from participating in *Stress Less*.

• Read out loud and together Psalm 23. Share the words and phrases that were most meaningful to you. Discuss why this scripture is so comforting.

• Talk about the idea of being balanced and how this relates to stress. See the "Be a Star" group activity below.

• Discuss the qualities of a spiritually healthy person. Talk about the person that you thought about as the individual who most demonstrates these qualities.

• Share what you learned from completing the "Spiritual Wellness Assessment and Worksheet."

• Discuss the relationship between spirituality and stress.

• What was the one thing from chapter seven that you did to simplify your life?

• What was the most important thing you learned from the first seven chapters of *Stress Less*?

Group Activities

Be a Star

The leader draws a large five-pointed star on newsprint or on the chalkboard and labels each point of the star—physical health, mental health, emotional health, spiritual health, and social health. Ask each participant to draw a star on a piece of paper with each tip drawn in relationship to the amount of time and commitment they devote to that aspect of their health. For example, the physical health point may be very small if you do not take time for exercise and eating right. The social point might be very large if you spend a lot of time socializing with friends. The ideal is a well-balanced star in all five dimensions of health.

In small groups of two or three, share one thing you do to stay healthy in each of these five dimensions of health. Come together as a large group. Tell one idea that you learned from someone in your small group. A couple of participants might be willing to share their star with the group and explain why they drew it as they did.

Powerful Perceptions

In chapter four, you made a list of things you love. On a large sheet of paper or on the chalkboard, come forward and write some things from your list. Discuss how seeing the blessings rather than the burdens can change your perspective. Share one experience from this week in which changing perspectives resulted in less stress.

For Next Week

Remind everyone to read *Section Two—Understanding Stress,* chapters 8 through 14. Suggest that participants read one short chapter a day and spend some time with the "Start Today" and "Evening Reflections" material at the end of each chapter.

Thanksgiving

Close today's session with one or two volunteers reading the prayer of thanksgiving they wrote for chapter six.

Soul Soother

Do a Soul Soother activity. (Remember to ask two or three volunteers to plan this activity each week.) Consider these ideas:
- Listen to a relaxation tape for five or ten minutes.
- Read Psalm 23 together, followed by five minutes of quiet mindfulness.

Session Three—Understanding Stress

Discussion Ideas

• Talk about your results from the "Ardell Wellness Stress Test." Discuss some of the major stressors in your life. Ask for suggestions and ideas from the group on ways that have worked for them in dealing with these stressors.

• Bring your stress journals and discuss what you learned from this activity. Were you able to identify any patterns?

• Talk about anger.

• Discuss the most meaningful scripture that you read this week. What did this scripture mean to you?

• Share together some of the irrational things you worry about.

• What are some of the daily hassles that cause you stress? Brainstorm as a group on ways to eliminate these hassles from your life.

• Discuss some of the people that you stress and how you are stressful to them. Talk about possible ways you could change to help reduce the stress to others.

Group Activities
Feeling creative?
Form small groups and make up some new verses to add to *I Think I'll Just Go Take a Snooze* on page 36. Share your creations with the group.

Stress Overload
Make a group list of some of the negative physical effects of stress that different class members have experienced. Pray for God's help in relieving these specific symptoms of stress.

Watch Your Worries Go Up In Smoke
Write down on slips of paper some of your irrational worries. Gather around a campfire and name the worry as you toss it in the fire. Why not roast some marshmallow while you are having fun?

No campfire? Then place a garbage can in the middle of the room and shoot baskets with your wadded-up worries. Feel the pressure of unnecessary worry lift.

Ask an Expert
Invite a nurse to class. Ask the nurse to check blood pressures and pulse rates. Talk about how stress affects health.

For Next Week
Remind everyone to read **Section Three—Stress Relievers,** chapters 15 through 21. Suggest that participants read one short chapter a day and spend some time with the "Start Today" and "Evening Reflections" material at the end of each chapter.

Soul Soother
As a group, do a Soul Soother. How about taking a walk together? Finish with some gentle, stress-relieving stretches. See page 77 for the Stretch Break.

Session Four—Stress Relievers

Discussion Ideas

• Talk about the different stress relievers that you learned this week. Which ones worked best for you?

• Discuss different types of exercise. Share ideas on how to incorporate exercise into your life on a regular basis. Talk about ways to eliminate barriers to exercise. Think about forming a church walking or stretching group. For a description of different types of exercise and important information on starting an exercise program, see *Health Yourself, Participant's Handbook* by Margie Hesson (Abingdon Press, 1995).

• Discuss the cognitive distortions from chapter 21 this week. Give some real-life examples.

• Review the cognitive techniques from chapter 21. How did they work for you?

• Talk about your favorite way to pamper yourself.

• Discuss the relationship between discipline in your physical life and discipline in your spiritual life. How will becoming more disciplined in one area help you in the other?

• Close today's session by sharing some Breath Prayers (see page 90). Discuss areas of your life where you need God's healing and refreshing breath of life.

Group Activities
Stress Relievers
Bring a mat or blanket to class so you can practice a couple of stress relievers together. Have someone guide the group in deep breathing and progressive muscle relaxation.

Exercise Break

Do some gentle stretches together. Each person can lead the group in their favorite stretch. Go for a short walk.

Mental Imagery

If you wrote your own mental imagery story (see page 85), consider reading it to the group as they relax. How about forming groups of three or four and writing a brief mental imagery together? Or, if each of you wrote a story you could make copies for each person in class and compile them as a gift to one another.

Ask an Expert

Invite an exercise expert to talk about the different types of exercise. Discuss the advantages of each type. Develop an exercise plan.

For Next Week

Remind everyone to read *Section Four—Seven Keys to Stress Less Living,* chapters 22 through 28. Suggest that participants read one short chapter a day and spend some time with the "Start Today" and "Evening Reflections" material at the end of each chapter.

Soul Soother

Do your Soul Soother together.

Session Five—Seven Keys to Stress Less Living

Discussion Ideas
- Share with the group your idea for an adventure. Maybe some of you could join together to plan for an adventure.

- Talk about the old Moroccan proverb, "Trust in God, but tie your camel tight." How do you balance self-responsibility with faith that God is in control?

- Discuss the role that food plays in your life. Do you use food as a pacifier? What did you learn from your Daily Food Diary assignment?

- In chapter 25 you learned about the importance of solitude. Discuss how you are doing about making time for yourself. Share with the group your plan for a day off.

- Discuss the power of Amy's story about laughter as good medicine from chapter 26, pages 119-20.

- Share a joyful experience from this week.

- Volunteer to share the paragraph you wrote about what it means to have God guiding your life (see page 125).

Group Activities
Laughter Is Good Medicine
You read this week about the importance of fun and laughter. Plan for some fun today. Everyone could share his or her favorite joke or you could come up with some ideas for playing together. Who said playing is just for kids? Or be silly—have everyone wear a goofy hat or tell an embarrassing story.

Reflection
Today is your last *Stress Less* class. Share with the group the most important part of this program for you. Flip through the daily readings. Which one seemed to speak most to you? Why?

The Journey Continues

Talk about your "Stress Less Contract." How do you plan to change your life so you can enjoy more abundant living?

Support

Stand in a circle. Place your hands on your own shoulders and give yourself a brief massage. Next, turn to your right and give a shoulder massage to the person in front of you. After a few minutes, turn around and give a brief massage to the person who was just massaging you. Talk about the differences between massaging yourself, receiving a massage from someone else, and giving a massage to another. Think about the idea of feeling connected and supportive.

Over the last four weeks each of you has shared. You have given. You have received. Remain in a circle as you close today's session and offer prayers of thanks and praise.

What Next?

If your group would like to learn more about healthy living from the Christian perspective, consider Margie Hesson's *Health Yourself, Ten Weeks to a Healthier Lifestyle** as your next small group study resource.

Health Yourself is a ten-week program for Christians seeking a healthy lifestyle. The participant's handbook provides practical information on healthy eating, exercise, and emotional well-being as well as fifty-six daily devotions. The leader's guide provides step-by-step session plans and reproducible handouts to support each lesson.

Health Yourself uses faith, fun, facts, and fellowship to focus on the spiritual, physical, mental, emotional, and social aspects of persons for a powerful approach to behavior change—change to a healthier lifestyle.

* *Health Yourself, Ten Weeks to a Healthier Lifestyle* by Margie Hesson,
  Copyright © 1995 by Abingdon Press
  Participant's Handbook ISBN 0-687-00305-9; Leader's Guide ISBN 0-687-00304-0